My Personal Prayer Diary

My Personal Prayer Diary

Compiled and Written by

Catherine Marshall
and
Leonard LeSourd

HODDER AND STOUGHTON
LONDON SYDNEY AUCKLAND TORONTO

". . . if ever he [any man] consciously directs his prayers 'Not to what I think Thou art, but to what Thou knowest Thyself to be', our [Satan's] situation is, for the moment, desperate."

The Screwtape Letters
C. S. LEWIS

Extracts from *A Diary of Private Prayer* by John Baillie are reproduced by kind permission of Oxford University Press.

British Library Cataloguing in Publication Data

Marshall, Catherine and LeSourd, Leonard
My personal prayer diary.
1. Prayer-books
I. Title   II. LeSourd, Leonard
242'.8   BV245

ISBN 0 340 25324 X

Foreword

It sounds strange to say that the book which literally taught me to pray consists mostly of blank pages!

I felt desperate the day I first encountered Catherine Marshall's *Personal Prayer Diary*. Clutching my Christmas token I dived into the book shop in search of something that would revitalise my almost non-existent devotional life! With six kids, two foster children and an invalid mother my prayers were mostly gasps for help as I galloped to the next assignment!

The name – Catherine Marshall – caught my eye at once. I had devoured all her books in my more leisured days, but this one was different. She simply supplied a verse, and short prayer or meditation for each day and left the rest of the page blank. The reader was supposed to write down what they wanted to ask God, and then, when He answered, to fill in His response beside their request.

Soon I found myself sharing the book with my early morning tea, condensing my daily needs to a sentence or even a word. In no time I was staggered to find just how many miracles God actually performed.

I don't find prayer easy, I'm the practical type who likes to see tangible results for my efforts. Prayers float away into space and are lost, but seeing them written down in black and white and their answers added later, has helped me realise just how real and powerful prayer is. My faith and enthusiasm grew enormously as my vague, woolly prayers became specific and concise and I actually began to *expect* God to answer them!

At the end of each month Catherine leaves a page for a summary. I can drift away from God so quickly, but the discipline of regular 'spiritual stock taking' helps me spot early danger signals, as well as filling my heart with praise at all God has achieved.

Catherine Marshall's quotations, comments and prayers are a wonderful adjunct to deeper Bible study. But at times when I have been too busy, stressed or ill for anything more, they have been my lifeline. I am delighted this book is being republished and I hope it will mean as much to you as it has to me.

Jennifer Rees Larcombe
June 1988

Acknowledgments

We are indebted to Alice Watkins for her research into prayer books and various Bible translations and for tirelessly typing and retyping the prayers as we revised them; to Edith Marshall for her research and helpful contributions. We also wish to thank Page Bailey, Betty Schneider and Louise Gibbons of the Chosen Books staff for prayer suggestions and typing help. And to Patricia Fletter of San Diego, California, who wrote a letter to us with the suggestion that we publish a prayer diary.

One Hour, a Bible and
an Open Mind

About the middle of my sophomore year at Agnes Scott
College, I began keeping a journal, writing in it at the end of
each day. I had already discovered that for me thoughts and
inspirations flowed most readily at the point of a pencil.
Ideas, convictions, emotions, yearnings were bubbling and
seething, crying out for an outlet. The journal supplied that.

As the years went on, the first journal became a shelf full
of them containing a potpourri of everything imaginable—
the recordings of external events and concerns, fragments of
poetry and quotations, vivid descriptions of people and
places, Scripture promises, the record of my personal gropings for answers.

Meanwhile, towards the end of March 1943 came a
watershed event in my life, therefore also for the journals.
Declining health sent me to Johns Hopkins Hospital Clinic
in Baltimore for a complete physical examination. After all
the tests and X-rays were completed, the day came to hear
the specialist's report.

Moments before I was to walk into the doctor's office to
get that verdict, God spoke to me. It was a gentle prepar-
ation for what lay ahead. I sensed that the news would not
be good.

Passing years have blurred the exact words of the message,
but the gist of it remains clear: "Body is irretrievably tied
to spirit: physical health will always be dependent on
spiritual health. For you, beginning every day with a quiet
time with Me is essential."

The message was given in such imperative terms that it

obscured the fact that the Lord was also preparing me for the doctor's report. For the news was grim. I was to go home and go to bed—full time.

During the next year and a half there was plenty of leisure for that morning "Quiet Hour". My gropings after truth were intensified by immense need. The journals ballooned apace.

In the years since then I have not always kept faith with this daily lifeline. But whenever I slip, I know what the trouble is and what to do about it.

When my husband, Peter Marshall, died so suddenly at forty-six, the journal notations recorded all the elements of heartache, fear and discouragement experienced by any young widow with a nine-year-old son, together with the answers given me.

Then after ten years of widowhood, in 1959, Leonard LeSourd came into my life, bringing the need to call from me a new dimension of motherhood for his three young children. Inevitably the joining of two homes containing four children would bring Len and me a multitude of new problems. Shortly after returning from our honeymoon, these adjustments threatened to overwhelm us.

How could we cope with the rebellion of a nineteen-year-old son away at Yale, the hostility of a ten-year-old daughter, and the discipline of two young boys, three and six, who had for years been subject to a series of housekeepers? Not to mention moving into a new house in a new community, seeking the right help, solving two career adjustments and coping with myriad needs of family and relatives?

Aware that I was arising early each day, Len became curious. "Long ago I learned," I explained, "that I need time with the Lord every morning if I'm to keep my head above the water. For me, it's a must."

Len looked thoughtful. "That would be good for me too. We could set the alarm for thirty minutes earlier."

I shook my head. "That's not enough time."

He looked at me incredulously. But he too soon discovered that to fill our thoughts with the power and wisdom of Scripture, meditate on that and pray adequately for our concerns, we needed a full hour before the children were up and the daily turmoil and confusion began.

Three simple purchases were made one winter day almost twenty years ago. I bought a small electric percolator, a timing device that would start it percolating whenever we set it, and a brown notebook for Len. These items were to shape our early morning hours for many years.

It was Len who began to keep a prayer log; we had so many prayer requests that we could not keep them all in our minds. Just as the "Quiet Hour" had been essential to me alone, now it became the stabilizing factor in our marriage. It has provided the setting in which we seek to grow in faith, to come closer to God and to build inner strength to withstand the fierce storms and satanic onslaughts which every person faces in life.

The basic tools are notebook, pen or pencil, and a Bible. Additional tools such as a concordance, Bible commentaries and books on faith and prayer can all be helpful.

We conceived of this resource book as a way for an individual or a couple to get started on a devotional programme that can lift and strengthen life. In a marriage, one can be the recorder, as Len was in our case, or both can keep separate spiritual diaries.

These are difficult, terrifying times. A simple faith, called upon only in emergencies, is not enough today. The attack on morals, religious beliefs and standards of decency are shattering those who have no inner protection. Desperately we need the armour of God. But how can we put on the armour unless we are knowledgeable about the equipment provided us in the very real world of the spirit? Daily food in absorbing the Word of God is just as much needed as food for our bodies; daily communication face-to-face with the One who can help us and rescue us is indispensable.

An hour each day, a favourite translation of the Bible that you make your own by marking it, and the use of a resource book like this one can start you on a prayer journey that will turn your problems into highways and make your life an adventure.

CATHERINE MARSHALL

How This Prayer Diary Can Help You Grow Spiritually

I began making lists as a college student at Ohio Wesleyan back in the late '30s: papers to write, personal items needed, girls to call for dates. Three years as a pilot in the Air Corps during World War II interrupted this process, but it began again when I became an editor at Guideposts Magazine in 1946.

The years peeled off, Guideposts grew steadily through the late '40s and '50s. Each week began with a list of things to do: conferences with writers, articles to edit, staff meetings, family needs.

Early summer 1959 found me in a major crisis. A single parent with three children to rear, I went through eight housekeepers in two years. I simply could not handle my job and meet the needs of my young children alone. Something had to be done. Yet how could I know what God wanted for me? Or whether His plan could include a second marriage?

Alone in my bedroom late one night I closed my eyes and prayed. "Lord, what about it? I can't go on like this. Do You have anyone in mind for me?"

One name immediately popped into my thoughts—Catherine Marshall.

Surely, Lord, that isn't from You, I thought. I knew Catherine professionally but had placed her in a special category: *highly spiritual*. Her marriage to Peter Marshall had been movingly portrayed to millions in articles, a best-selling book and a very successful motion picture.

However, in case the Lord really *was* guiding me, I made

11

a date to see Catherine in Washington, D.C., letting her think that this meeting was for professional reasons. Though I found her warm and feminine, it was the façade of the professional woman that she presented to me.

I decided to try once more. This time for ten hours straight we talked on a summer day as we walked through Rock Creek Park west of Washington, picnicked alone and drove along Skyline Drive. There was an incredible meshing together of beliefs, thoughts and experiences. Four months later we were married.

As Catherine has already written, soon after our marriage we faced a staggering array of problems and difficulties to work out. Catherine teasingly suggested that I needed a list to keep track of my lists. Our early morning prayer time together became the anchor point of each day.

What a joy to be awakened each day by the gentle sound and pleasant aroma of coffee percolating! By the time the coffee was ready, we were each surrounded by Bibles, books, my new brown notebook and pencils. We each read quietly for the first half hour (sometimes in separate spots) then spent the second half hour on prayer work.

For it really was work. Most of the entries focused on Peter (nineteen), Linda (ten), Chester (six) and Jeff (three). The log that first day in our new home in Chappaqua, New York contained these items:

Prayer Requests—December 15, 1959

1. That we locate the right housekeeper who can cook and who enjoys taking care of children.
2. That Catherine will know how and when she is to continue writing *Christy*.
3. That Peter do more work and less playing around at Yale.
4. That Linda will be less emotional about the clothes we ask her to wear and more interested in her studies.
5. That Chester stop fighting with his brother and accept his new home situation.
6. That we get Jeff toilet-trained.

Dozens of additional prayer requests filled the pages of the days that followed: a close relative with a drinking problem, a stealing problem at the office, a broken relationship with a neighbour, tensions with in-laws, guidance as to which church we should belong to, financial decisions involving family members. The items went on and on.

One day the request for the right housekeeper was answered. Through my mother we learned about Lucy, who made it possible for Catherine to resume her work on the novel *Christy*. In a separate page I wrote at the top: *Prayer Answers*. Underneath I made a notation about Lucy—and the date she began to work for us.

Soon we learned more about answers to prayer: specific requests yield precise answers. We didn't just ask for help with the house, we asked for live-in help, someone who would be warm, comfortable, a good cook, someone who liked children. We also discovered that unless we actually wrote down the *answers* to our prayers, we tended to accept them as occurring just in the natural course of events. With written notes marking prayer answers we found ourselves with deeper and more articulate gratitude. Not only that, watching those answers pile up, being able to look back in the log and see how ingeniously God had answered our prayer requests was a marvellous stimulus to faith.

The decision to arise early each morning for a time of prayer and Bible study was the turning point in our marriage, helping us resolve day-by-day tensions and upsets. Prayer forced us to face up to each situation. We could duck some problems for a while but not for long. The morning prayer period was also the time for an honest sharing of feelings between us. I discovered early that if I tried to present a controversial matter the night before, the adrenalin started flowing, the talk became charged and Catherine would go sleepless until dawn. Early morning in a prayer atmosphere was the time for confrontations.

What I learned from this prayer experience together began to shape my role as a husband. At the beginning of our marriage I had made two wrong assumptions. The first was that Catherine was better equipped to be the spiritual leader of our home since she knew more than I did about the Bible and was more articulate in prayer. But I soon learned, to my surprise, that these qualities do not qualify a wife for spiritual uthority over her husband and children.

My second wrong assumption was that Catherine wanted this role. Not only did she resist it instinctively, but she did not want to go against the scriptural position that it is the husband's role to be "prophet" and "priest" for his own household.

Yet she also sensed that it would be a mistake to push me into a spiritual posture I did not want to assume. I belonged to the masculine school which held that because women were in the home more than men, they had better opportunities to provide children with religious teaching. When Catherine balked at the role I tried to assign her, the matter became one of our chief prayer concerns in our early morning time together.

It did not take me long to realize that unless I became the spiritual head of our home, Chester and Jeff would consider religion as something for the womenfolk. It was frightening to see how my sons copied everything I did: mannerisms, speech, attitudes towards work, food, church, sports. When I said grace and led the family prayer time, they were soon praying too, as if it were the natural thing to do. Despite my almost "bread and potatoes" prayers, I soon found myself quite comfortable in the role as spiritual head of our home.

And so our morning prayer period has set the tone and direction for every day in our twenty years of marriage. We turn over our problems to the Lord. We commit ourselves to Him. We are submitted to each other. For two people with strong individualistic natures who can disagree on all manner of issues, the oneness that comes during our early morning time together is the stabilizing factor in our marriage.

How To Use This Diary

1. Set aside an hour each day, if possible, early in the morning.

2. Find a quiet place away from interruptions for prayer, reading and meditation.
3. The basics are a Bible, pen or pencil, and a prayer log. Additional resources recommended: concordance, Bible commentary, a recent translation of the Bible to go with the King James or RSV editions.
4. Use the Scripture references and prayers in this book as guidelines, improvising or adding to them as you see fit.
5. Seek to memorize one verse of Scripture each day. Three-by-five cards can be used to write down the verse. Carry each verse with you all day long and refer to it at free moments. In a matter of months you will have stored up a treasury of Bible wisdom which can be called upon in all kinds of situations.
6. For couples I suggest a prayer procedure as follows: (a) talk over the people and situations you are concerned about until you decide how you want to pray; (b) then pray aloud, together; (c) one or both should then record the prayers in this book.
7. When a prayer has been answered, record the answer by date. If you are not sure of the exact date, include it in the monthly summary page.
8. Prayer work is the main purpose of this volume, but many will want to make daily notations of business and social events, including travel.
9. If you want to deal with a certain problem area in your life, check the listing of themes by date covered in the index and adjust the prayers and Bible verses to fit your schedule.
10. At the end of the year go back over each month, tally the results and write a yearly prayer summary in the pages so designated at the end of this volume. If you stay with it day by day, week by week, I believe the Lord will not only give you an adventuresome year, He will honour your faithfulness and bless your life.

LEONARD LESOURD

January 1

God's Word to me: Prepare ye the way of the Lord, make straight in the desert a highway for our God.

Isaiah 40:3

Prayer-meditation: Prepare my heart, Lord, to receive afresh the King of Kings. Purge me with Your Holy Spirit that He may find a clean, warm and responsive abode in me. Help me to face the new year with courage, enthusiasm and faith.

My prayer requests:	*God's answers:*

CLEANSING OF THE HEART

January 2

God's Word to me: Create in me a clean heart, O God, and put a new and right spirit within me.

Psalm 51:10 (RSV)

Prayer-meditation: Lord Jesus, we come to You now as little children. Dress us again in clean pinafores; make us tidy again, once more with the tidiness of true remorse and confession. O wash our hearts, that they may be clean again. Make us to know the strengthening joys of the Spirit and the newness of life which only You can give.

PETER MARSHALL

My prayer requests:

God's answers:

January 3

God's Word to me: He that hath My commandments, and keepeth them, he it is that loveth Me ...

John 14:21
(Read also John 14:18–27)

Prayer-meditation: Some unknown saint long ago penned these words: "Perfect obedience would be perfect happiness if only we had perfect confidence in the power we were obeying." Yet, Father, I cannot trust You *like that* unless I know You as You really are. I ask now for that kind of unfolding friendship with You.

My prayer requests:	*God's answers:*

THE NATURE OF GOD

January 4

God's Word to me: Why do you ask Me about what is good? There is only One Who is good.

Matthew 19:17 (NIV)
(Read also Psalm 107:1–9)

Prayer-meditation: Father, I confess that I have sometimes maligned You by questioning why a loving God would allow some of the awful tragedies in our world. Or under a cloak of piety and resignation to Your will, I have attributed black deeds to You which even simple good will would preclude.

I would now rest on Jesus' own Word, His pledge to me, that His Father and my Father is good, incapable of anything but goodness.

My prayer requests:

God's answers:

January 5

God's Word to me: Yes, from the time of the first existence of day and from this day forth I am He, and there is no one who can deliver out of My hand. I will work and who can hinder or reverse it?

Isaiah 43:13 (AMPLIFIED)

Prayer-meditation:
　　As the marsh-hen secretly builds on the watery sod,
　　Behold I will build me a nest on the greatness of God.
　　　　　SIDNEY LANIER

Father, Your greatness includes limitless power, perfect peace, unerring guidance and all Your grace and strength to draw upon. Still I hesitate. Here I am living off the crumbs of Your bounty when I could have the whole loaf.

O Father, enlarge my vision. Give me faith.

My prayer requests:	*God's answers:*

January 6

God's Word to me: He who did not spare His own Son but gave Him up for us all, will He not also give us all things with Him?

Romans 8:32 (RSV)

Prayer-meditation: What glorious assurance that everything God asks us to do is for our own good and joy and best interests—not just "spiritual" good, but good as we earthly creatures understand it! It is an adventure to test this out for ourselves in daily life; to try obeying those inner nudges —though we may not at the time, understand. Then we get proof after proof of God's love and watch-care.

Lord, I would embark today on this adventure of prac-tising Your presence during every waking hour, trusting Your selfless love for me.

My prayer requests:	*God's answers:*

January 7

God's Word to me: If thou wilt walk in My ways, to keep My statutes and My commandments . . . then I will lengthen thy days.
1 Kings 3:14

Prayer-meditation: I was meditating today, Lord, on how many I know who died early in life and violently because they violated Your laws. Show me how to communicate this principle to the young and the careless.

My prayer requests:	*God's answers:*

January 8

God's Word to me: Be still, and know that I am God.

Psalm 46:10

Prayer-meditation:
> Where cross the crowded ways of life,
> Where sound the cries of race and clan,
> Above the noise of selfish strife,
> We hear Thy voice, O Son of man!
>
> O Master, from the mountainside,
> Make haste to heal these hearts of pain,
> Among these restless throngs abide,
> O tread the city's streets again.

FRANK M. NORTH

My prayer requests:

God's answers:

January 9

God's Word to me: By the word of the Lord the heavens were made, and all their host by the breath of His mouth.

Psalm 33:6 (RSV)
(Read also John 1:1–3; Colossians 1:15–17)

Prayer-meditation: Lord, the creative power of Your spoken Word is awesome to me. And I begin to see that You have shared with all Your children this startling, creative (or destructive) power of words. This day enable me to use this sacred trust aright.

My prayer requests:	God's answers:

January 10

God's Word to me: . . . He has granted to us His precious and very great promises, that through these you may escape from the corruption that is in the world . . .

2 Peter 1:4 (RSV)

Prayer-meditation: Since God cannot lie (Titus 1:2) and since He is bound by His own nature and by His Word to keep His promises (1 Kings 8:56), I see that Scripture is a veritable treasure chest of promises to claim for my every need. Help me to use these days to accumulate my own cherished collection of these great promises.

My prayer requests:	*God's answers:*

January 11

God's Word to me: So shall My word be that goeth forth out of My mouth: it shall not return unto me void; but it shall accomplish that which I please...

Isaiah 55:11
(Read also John 10:35)

Prayer-meditation: Gratefully, I accept Your Word as bedrock truth—a final anchor point in this confused and troubled world. Speak now, directly to me, Lord, out of Your Word.

My prayer requests:	*God's answers:*

January 12

God's Word to me: Thy Word have I hid in mine heart, that I might not sin against thee.

Psalm 119:11

Prayer-meditation: Hiding Your Word in my heart must mean memorizing many of the treasure chest of precious promises in Your Word. When I meet that condition, then I have Your assurance, Lord, that the claiming of these promises will be a bulwark and protection for me. Help me to get on with it, Lord.

My prayer requests:	*God's answers:*

January 13

God's Word to me: . . . weeping may endure for a night, but joy cometh in the morning.

Psalm 30:5

Prayer-meditation: Lord, we can stand almost anything when we know it to be temporary. Even in the midst of my weeping, when I look into Your eyes, I always experience the lift to my spirit of Your light touch: "Why are you so troubled? There's nothing here I can't handle!" O Lord Jesus, thank You for the gift of Your clear-eyed perspective. It is priceless to me.

My prayer requests:	*God's answers:*

PRAYER FOR FORGIVENESS

January 14

God's Word to me: ... if we walk in the light, as He is in the light, we have fellowship with one another, and the blood of Jesus His Son cleanses us from all sin.

1 John 1:7 (RSV)

Prayer-meditation:

O unapproachable Light, how can I fold these guilty
   hands before Thee?
How can I pray to Thee with lips that have spoken false
   and churlish words?
... an unruly tongue:
A fretful disposition:
An unwillingness to bear the burdens of others:
An undue willingness to let others bear my
   burdens:
... Fine words hiding shabby thoughts:
A friendly face masking a cold heart.

JOHN BAILLIE

O Lord, have mercy!

My prayer requests:

God's answers:

January 15

God's Word to me: And when He had sent them away, He departed into a mountain to pray.

Mark 6:46

Prayer-meditation: Jesus' earthly life as recorded in the gospels has so much to teach me in the matter of priorities. For Him, prayer with His Father had top priority. This alone would pull Him away from those still unhealed or in need (Luke 4:42, 43). Jesus used prayer: for regular communion with God (Mark 1:35); to learn God's will—the prayer of decision (Luke 22:41, 42); for refreshment of body and spirit (Mark 6:46, 47).

Lord, teach me about the perfect balance You demonstrated between "busyness" and quietness, between service and prayer.

My prayer requests:	*God's answers:*

January 16

God's Word to me: You do not have, because you do not ask.

James 4:2 (RSV)

Prayer-meditation: Jesus assured us that our Father knows what we need before we ask Him (Matthew 6:8). Why then should we pray? Because in giving us free will, God made the fulfilling of His plans dependent upon man's co-operation. Then He gave us the privilege of being creators in partnership with the Creator Himself. This means that the whole thrust of God's nature is always positive—never negative.

Father, I am ashamed that so many of my prayer requests are negative—to get rid of something. Help me from now on to get on with the thrust of creativity, moving always upward.

My prayer requests: | *God's answers:*

January 17

God's Word to me: Likewise, ye husbands, dwell with them according to knowledge, giving honour unto the wife, as unto the weaker vessel, and as being heirs together of the grace of life; that your prayers be not hindered.

1 Peter 3:7

Prayer-meditation: Lord, are you saying that an unharmonious relationship between husband and wife will hinder prayer? *Being heirs together of the grace of life* is such a beautiful picture of a marriage that I will hold it before me in all my prayers for marriage problems.

My prayer requests:	*God's answers:*

PRAYER IN SECRET

January 18

God's Word to me: . . . when thou prayest, enter into thy closet, and when thou hast shut thy door, pray to thy Father which is in secret; and thy Father which seeth in secret shall reward thee openly.

Matthew 6:6
(*Read also Mark 7:36; Matthew 9:30*)

Prayer-meditation: Lord, here You are instructing us in a principle, one of God's immutable laws of the universe: there is additional spiritual power in secrecy. Or conversely, creative power is dissipated by talking about it too soon.

This gives yet another exciting dimension to prayer. What adventure to enter into a secret prayer conspiracy with You and then see the joyous result exhibited for all to see!

My prayer requests:	*God's answers:*

January 19

God's Word to me: . . . pray constantly . . . I desire then that in every place the men should pray . . .

1 Thessalonians 5:17; 1 Timothy 2:8 (RSV)

Prayer-meditation: Our friend John has taught us something important about prayer. Instead of saying, as we often have, "We really should pray about so-and-so" (meaning sometime) or "Let's remember to pray about _____ ", invariably, no matter what we are doing at the time, John will say, "Let's pray *now*"—and proceed to do so. How else can we pray "in every place"?

My prayer requests: *God's answers:*

DEPRESSION

January 20

God's Word to me: . . . Arise and eat . . . Rise, let us be going . . .
1 Kings 19:5; Matthew 26:46
(*Read also 1 Kings 19:1–18*)

Prayer-meditation: Being depressed sometimes is simply part of our humanness. Otherwise, we would have no capacity for joy, inspiration, and exaltation. Thus the Bible is peppered with accounts of the depressed: Elijah, Job, King David, Jonah, Joshua, Jesus' apostles.

Thank You, Father, for giving me a prescription for my depression: I am to stop analysing myself, rise, and perform the next commonplace task at hand "as unto the Lord". Thank you that as I take this initiative, You will return perspective and joy to me.

My prayer requests:	*God's answers:*

January 21

God's Word to me: ... until Christ be formed in you.
Galatians 4:19 (RSV)

Prayer-meditation: O Lord, I do not need patience or self-control, or even love today; what I really need is You ... Your life lived out through mine until Your very likeness is reproduced in my life. And then You will be everything that I need: patience ... self-control ... love, and all the other fruits. I praise You that You are the One answer to my every need—Jesus.

My prayer requests:	*God's answers:*

January 22

God's Word to me: He [God] is the source of your life in Christ Jesus . . . therefore, as it is written, "Let him who boasts, boast of the Lord."

1 Corinthians 1:30, 31 (RSV)

Prayer-meditation: God has performed what we could not accomplish for ourselves: He has put us into Christ.

Lord Jesus, You have made the way for our deliverance from sin by our death in Christ. And You have even seen to it that we have been placed in Him already. There is nothing left for us to do but rejoice in the marvellous excellency of Your redemption.

My prayer requests: *God's answers:*

January 23

God's Word to me: She has done a beautiful thing to me.

Mark 14:6 (RSV)
(Read also Mark 14:3–9)

Prayer-meditation: O Lord, grant me the satisfaction of pleasing You; not in work *for* You primarily, but in relationship *with* You. I would be like the woman spending herself totally, wastefully, on Your behalf. Cause my single-minded goal to be that of satisfying You first. Then will my longing heart be satisfied in a love relationship with You.

My prayer requests: | *God's answers:*

January 24

God's Word to me: If you continue in my word, you are truly my disciples, and you will know the truth, and the truth will make you free . . . So if the Son makes you free, you will be free indeed.
John 8:31, 32, 36 (RSV)

Prayer-meditation: O Lord, You of all men, were the most free because You were totally free of self-love.

Free us, Lord, from the darkness of lonely isolation. Free us from everything that holds us in crippling fear and worry to a childlike abandonment to our Father. Free us, O Holy Spirit, to make choices in terms of God, not ourselves, as our centre.

My prayer requests: | *God's answers:*

January 25

God's Word to me: And now He [Jesus] can help those who are tempted, because He Himself was tempted and suffered.

Hebrews 2:18 (TEV)

Prayer-meditation: To be tempted is not synonymous with sinning; rather temptation is the inheritance of the human race. Further, we are tempted only by those things of which we are capable and even susceptible. Therefore, if we live at a base level of the physical and material, this will be the level of our temptations.

Lord, help me to recognize temptation as a mark of Your trust in me to grow above it—not to be ensnared by it.

My prayer requests:	*God's answers:*

TEMPTATION

January 26

God's Word to me: Blessed is the man that endureth temptation: for when he is tried, he shall receive the crown of life, which the Lord hath promised to them that love Him.

James 1:12

Prayer-meditation: Temptation is not something we can escape. For the Christian it may come in the opportunity to take a less effective but shorter route to accomplish our highest goal. This only cheapens the achievement and leaves the Christian unfulfilled.

Lord, thank You for the encouragement to keep to Your wonderful plan for the building of my life regardless of the cost. For Lord, I greatly desire to attain the "Crown of Life".

My prayer requests:

God's answers:

January 27

God's Word to me: . . . each person is tempted when he is lured
and enticed by his own desire.

James 1:14 (RSV)
(Read also Matthew 4:1–11)

Prayer-meditation: Satan tailors his temptations to fit both
the taste and the capability of each of us: what is not attractive to *us* would obviously be no temptation at all; neither
would ambitions so far beyond us as to be ludicrous. Note
how even with Jesus this same pattern was followed: To the
Lord of glory Satan offered nothing less than "all the king-
doms of the world"!

Lord, give me an awareness that Satan knows *me*—my
tastes and particular ambitions—and along with that awareness give me Your strength in resisting him.

My prayer requests: | *God's answers:*

LOVE ONE ANOTHER

January 28

God's Word to me: Be kindly affectioned one to another with brotherly love; in honour preferring one another.

Romans 12:10

Prayer-meditation: Lord, I'm glad You said that. There have been times when I have so longed for a Christian brother or sister who would love me enough to be interested in sharing dreams and difficulties, joys and sorrows. Keep me sensitive, Father, to those who need my love.

My prayer requests:	God's answers:

January 29

God's Word to me: Draw nigh to God, and He will draw nigh to you.

James 4:8

Prayer-meditation: The Word is so simple, Lord. Why do I always try to make it complex? When I am feeling lost, alone, bereft, cannot feel Your presence—even when I am most reluctant to pray—that is precisely when I need most to draw nigh to you. I praise You for Your sure promise that when I do, You *will* respond, You *will* draw nigh to me.

My prayer requests:	*God's answers:*

DREAMS AND VISIONS

January 30

God's Word to me: And it shall come to pass afterward, that I will pour out My Spirit upon all flesh . . . your old men shall dream dreams, your young men shall see visions.

Joel 2:28
(Read also Acts 2:1–17)

Prayer-meditation: How marvellously You bridge the span of life for us, Lord. In our youth You paint brilliant pictures of opportunities full of stimulating challenge, needing the vigour of youth to achieve. Then when the strength of our flesh has diminished, gently You encourage us with dreams that continually refuel the bright light of hope.

My prayer requests:	*God's answers:*

January 31

God's Word to me: I can do all things in Him who strengthens me.
Philippians 4:13 (RSV)
(Read also Romans 8:2)

Prayer-meditation: Christ has changed all our "cannots" into "can dos".

O Lord, I have tasted a bit of the power of Your new life to overcome old ways. Through yielding to Your Spirit, You have enabled me to do things I never thought possible. For where I was bound before, now in You I am free. My strength is insufficient for the tasks You will call me to today, but the power that upholds the universe can handle all my needs. Keep me in the stream of Your strengthening, enabling life.

My prayer requests:	*God's answers:*

JANUARY SUMMARY

ENLARGE MY SPIRITUAL VISION

February 1

God's Word to me: Now therefore, I pray Thee, if I have found grace in Thy sight, shew me now Thy way that I may know Thee, that I may find grace in Thy sight . . .

Exodus 33:13
(Read also Exodus 33:11–19)

Prayer-meditation: As the Lord comforted and emboldened Moses, I too need reassurance and direction, Lord. Enlarge my spiritual vision that I may see Your presence and Your glory in all areas of my life.

My prayer requests:	God's answers:

February 2

God's Word to me: And God saw every thing that He had made, and, behold, it was very good . . . For every creature of God is good, and nothing to be refused, if it be received with thanksgiving: for it is sanctified by the Word of God and prayer.

Genesis 1:31; 1 Timothy 4:4, 5

Prayer-meditation:

Grant to us, O Father, the ability to see infinite value and importance in everything that You have made.

GLENN CLARK

My prayer requests:	*God's answers:*

February 3

God's Word to me: And it was at Jerusalem the feast of the dedication, and it was winter.

John 10:22

Prayer-meditation: Winter speaks of deadness of spirit. The spiritually dead crucified the Son of God! In the deadness of my spirit, Lord, come with Your resurrection power and healing in Your wings that I may be restored to what I was in You from the beginning.

My prayer requests: *God's answers:*

February 4

God's Word to me: Then I will restore her ... and make the dale of trouble a door of hope.

Hosea 2:15 (MOFFATT)
(Read also Genesis 45:1–8)

Prayer-meditation: It helps so much to know that before any event reaches us, God already has a plan by which He can bring good out of the difficulty (Romans 8:28). God wants to use trouble as the starting point for new creativity.

Father, how sorely I need this assurance, knowing that You are the only One who can make my dale of trouble a door of hope. I praise You that in the end, no evil can defeat the Lord of my life.

My prayer requests: | *God's answers:*

February 5

God's Word to me: But without faith it is impossible to please Him: for he that cometh to God must believe that He is . . . a rewarder of them that diligently seek Him.

Hebrews 11:6

Prayer-meditation: The apostles' cry to You, Lord Jesus, was "Give us more faith". They saw this as the most urgent need of their lives because of Your own attitude about it: healing depends on faith (Matthew 9:29; Luke 8:50); the forgiveness of sins comes through faith (Luke 7:50; 5:20). As You controlled the elements, You asked the disciples, "Where is your faith?" (Luke 18:8).

Teach me now, Lord, how to get the faith I sorely need.

My prayer requests:	*God's answers:*

February 6

God's Word to me: Looking unto Jesus the author and finisher of our faith ...

Hebrews 12:2
(Read also 1 Corinthians 12:9)

Prayer-meditation: Lord, I know that I can no more get on in my Christian life without faith than a fish can survive out of water.

Since the Apostle Paul tells us that faith can only come as a gift of the Holy Spirit, it occurs to me that I have never specifically asked for the gift of faith.

I ask now, Lord Jesus, and thank You for this great gift.

My prayer requests:	*God's answers:*

February 7

God's Word to me: So then faith cometh by hearing, and hearing by the Word of God.

Romans 10:17
(Read also Romans 10:8–17)

Prayer-meditation: This morning Your Word is telling me, Lord, that my faith can be nourished through two strong channels: Scripture and hearing Your Word proclaimed by those preachers who have been truly "sent" by You.

I see that I need Scripture because (1) I cannot claim God's promises for myself until I know what He has promised, and (2) because the Bible is the story of God's dealings with people like me.

Lead me, Lord, to those proclaimers of the Word who are the "sent" ones.

My prayer requests:

God's answers:

February 8

God's Word to me: Far better to rely on the Eternal than put faith in men.

Psalm 118:8 (MOFFATT)

Prayer-meditation: My tendency, Lord, is never to rely on God alone until circumstances force me to do so. How often I have said, "Of course I believe that God can do anything, but . . ." The "but" reveals that my faith has not gone beyond intellectual belief.

Show me one area today, Lord, where You want me to rely on You alone without trying to work out my own salvation.

My prayer requests:

God's answers:

February 9

God's Word to me: . . . for He [Jesus] knew what was in man.
John 2:25

Prayer-meditation:
It is, no doubt impossible to prevent his praying for his mother, but we [hell] have means of rendering the prayers innocuous. Make sure that they are always very "spiritual", that he is always concerned with the state of her soul and never with her rheumatism.

C. S. LEWIS

Lord Jesus, let me not fall into Satan's trap of pseudo-spirituality—more concerned about *my* high state spiritually than about the true needs of those around me.

My prayer requests:	*God's answers:*

THE CRY OF THE HUMAN HEART

February 10

God's Word to me: O my God, I cry in the daytime, but Thou hearest not; and in the night season, and am not silent.

Psalm 22:2

Prayer-meditation: My self-centredness causes me to cry out for this life, Jesus, to hold it as a "darling of my heart". Yet I remember that You said, "He who loses his life for My sake, shall have life eternal." Help me to desire You with my whole heart.

My prayer requests:	God's answers:

February 11

God's Word to me: Speak, Lord; for thy servant heareth.
1 Samuel 3:9, 10

Prayer-meditation: Lord, when I have spilled out to You my concerns and needs, my prayer has only just begun. What You have to say to me is of far more importance. Give me a listening, open heart perceptive to Your voice, ready to heed and to obey.

My prayer requests:	*God's answers:*

February 12

God's Word to me: And he said, Who art Thou, Lord?

Acts 9:5
(Read also Acts 7:58 and chapter 9)

Prayer-meditation: "Saul, Saul why persecutest thou Me?" Jesus knew his name! And in that question to him, Saul also recognized the voice of the Lord God. No wonder he trembled and fell on his face. His deeds, done in religious zeal were being denounced by the living God. But Saul recognized the voice of the One who was his heart's desire, and Jesus honoured his desire (motive) even though He denounced his works.

Lord, help me to listen first, that my works will not be in vain but a glory to Your Name.

My prayer requests:	*God's answers:*

February 13

God's Word to me: Knowing this, that the trying of your faith worketh patience .. . let patience have her perfect work . . .

James 1:3, 4

Prayer-meditation:

Deliver us, O Lord, from the foolishness of impatience. Let us not be in such a hurry as to run on without Thee. Slow us down, O Lord, that we may take time to think, time to pray, and time to find out Thy will.

PETER MARSHALL

My prayer requests:	*God's answers:*

February 14

God's Word to me: For the promise is unto you, and to your children . . . even as many as the Lord our God shall call.

Acts 2:39

Prayer-meditation: Thank You, Lord, for this promise. So many people who are coming to know You as Saviour have been parents for years. Now that You have given life to them, they are trying to make up in prayer all the lost years when they could have been teaching their children at Your feet. Thank You, Lord, for this encouragement.

My prayer requests:	*God's answers:*

February 15

God's Word to me: Children, obey your parents . . . for this is well-pleasing to the Lord.

Colossians 3:20 (AMPLIFIED)
Read also Matthew 15:3–6)

Prayer-meditation: Father, as I watch so many young working parents leave their toddlers at day-care centres, I wonder how these children can ever be able to know this teaching, much less obey it! Lord, so many of them scarcely know their parents. And their parents have not the time really to appreciate these little miracles of life You have entrusted to them.

O Father, I pray for these little ones, that they may know You and love You and follow You.

My prayer requests:	*God's answers:*

LIVING IN THE PRESENT

February 16

God's Word to me: Therefore do not be anxious about tomorrow
... Let the day's own trouble be sufficient for the day.

Matthew 6:34 (RSV)

Prayer-meditation:
> Lord, enable me and my family to savour today the joy
> of living in the present moment. "Let us perform our
> concerns and duties with laughter and kind faces, let
> cheerfulness abound with industry. Give us to go
> blithely on our business all this day ... Give us courage
> and gaiety and the quiet mind."

ROBERT LOUIS STEVENSON

My prayer requests:

God's answers:

February 17

God's Word to me: But sanctify the Lord God in your hearts: and be ready always to give an answer to every man that asketh you a reason of the hope that is in you with meekness and fear.

1 Peter 3:15

Prayer-meditation: Why are the lives of some Christians a more effective witness than others? Surely, Father, it is because the victorious ones have a conscious realization of Your indwelling presence. Discovering that You truly do indwell us revolutionizes our lives.

My prayer requests:

God's answers:

WITNESSING
February 18

God's Word to me: Now therefore go, and I will be with thy mouth, and teach thee what thou shalt say.

Exodus 4:12

Prayer-meditation: Lord, I am concerned about members of my family and friends whose lives are adrift because they do not know You. I am eager to present You to others. But my eagerness could be a hindrance and an offence unless fully controlled by Your Holy Spirit. So I ask that as You promised Moses to be with his mouth, so You will also be with me to give me the words to bring sinners to repentance and for the building up of believers.

My prayer requests:	*God's answers:*

February 19

God's Word to me: All scripture is given by inspiration of God, and is profitable for doctrine, for reproof, for correction, for instruction in righteousness: That the man of God may be perfect, thoroughly furnished unto all good works.

2 Timothy 3:16, 17

Prayer-meditation: I have observed, Father, that within our churches, as Christians witness to one another, we too often "minister" our own opinions. Lord, for myself and for my brothers and sisters in Christ, I ask that You will make us more conscious of the necessity to minister Your Word.

My prayer requests:	*God's answers:*

February 20

God's Word to me: . . . you shall receive power when the Holy Spirit has come upon you . . .

Acts 1:8 (RSV)

Prayer-meditation: Since I have no power of my own, I must rely on Your power, Lord Jesus, in order to be Your witnessing disciple. Prepare me for service, purge me of doubt, cleanse me of all impurity, and saturate me with Your Spirit.

My prayer requests:	*God's answers:*

February 21

God's Word to me: . . . And [the Samaritan] went to him, and bound up his wounds, pouring in oil and wine, and set him on his own beast, and brought him to an inn, and took care of him.

Luke 10:34

Prayer-meditation: Help me to be like that Samaritan, Lord, who did not seek counsel or approval from others before he reached out to help the injured man. Nor did he consider anything but the welfare of the one he helped. Instead he offered the same compassion You offered to the blind, the sick, the maimed and sin-weary people as You walked the roads of earth.

My prayer requests:	*God's answers:*

FAITH

February 22

God's Word to me: Woe to those who go down to Egypt for help and rely on horses, and trust in chariots because they are many and in horsemen because they are very strong, but they look not to the Holy One of Israel nor seek and consult the Lord!

Isaiah 31:1 (AMPLIFIED)

Prayer-meditation:

Our constant temptation is to trust in the "chariots of Egypt" or in other words, in earthly resources! We can *see* them; they are real and look substantial, while God's chariots are invisible and . . . it is hard to believe they are there.

HANNAH WHITALL SMITH

Father, You know my long-term concern about the salvation of _____. Open my eyes to see Your chariots rather than pinning my faith on earthly resources.

My prayer requests:	*God's answers:*

February 23

God's Word to me: This is the word of the Lord to Zerubbabel, saying, Not by might, nor by power, but by My Spirit, says the Lord of hosts.

For who are you, O great mountain [of human obstacles]?

Zechariah 4:6, 7 (AMPLIFIED)

Prayer-meditation: Lord, "might" and "power" seem so tangible and impressive. I confess to my shame that so often I do trust in "the chariots of Egypt", thus seeking to work out my own solutions rather than trusting the Lord of Hosts. Thank You that my particular mountain of human obstacles is no match for You.

My prayer requests:	*God's answers:*

February 24

God's Word to me: Why standest Thou afar off, O Lord? Why hidest Thou Thyself in times of trouble?

Psalm 10:1

Prayer-meditation:
> Eternal God . . . When the way seems dark before me,
>   give me grace to walk trustingly:
> When the distant scene is clouded, let me rejoice that at
>   least the next step is plain . . .
> When insight falters, let obedience stand firm:
> What I lack in faith, let me repay in love . . .
>   JOHN BAILLIE

My prayer requests: *God's answers:*

February 25

God's Word to me: ... a woman ... began to wash His feet with tears ...

Luke 7:37, 38
(Read also Luke 7:36–50)

Prayer-meditation: What a picture of depression! To reach the bottom; no self-esteem; no concern about becoming a public spectacle! But here was one who did not luxuriate in self-pity. She came to Jesus, poured out all her longings, her repentance for sin confessed by her actions, and found forgiveness and absolution beyond her wildest dreams.

"Thy faith hast saved thee; go in peace."

Thank You, Lord.

My prayer requests:	God's answers:

February 26

God's Word to me: ... . those that Thou gavest Me I have kept, and none of them is lost ...

John 17:12

Prayer-meditation: How reassuring it is, Father, to recognize that in spite of my failure to live up to Your Word, in spite of my surrendering to temptation on occasion, in spite of all the errancy of my humanity, I am still secure in You because of my relationship in Jesus.

Thank You for including in Scripture such people as Peter, Thomas, Mary Magdalene, James, John, David and many others who sinned but in repentance turned again to You and were restored to full fellowship with You. Thank You that I too may come this way.

My prayer requests:	*God's answers:*

February 27

God's Word to me: . . . in time past ye walked according to the course of this world . . . children of disobedience . . .

Ephesians 2:2

Prayer-meditation: This morning, Father, I would pray for _____, who is a new person in Christ Jesus. He/she is so new to Your kingdom and is not finding it easy to leave behind old habits, former companions, the stimuli and enticements of a world so at cross-purposes with Your purposes. Lord, strengthen _____ and other new struggling Christians as well. Help them quickly to recognize and relinquish to You all the enticements of the old life: certain types of music, reading and television; certain atmospheres, people—whatever. Be their "Remembrancer" who can alert them to the dangers and lead them to a safe place.

My prayer requests:	*God's answers:*

TRUST

February 28

God's Word to me: Brethren, I count not myself to have apprehended: but this one thing I do, forgetting those things which are behind, and reaching forth unto those things which are before . . .
Philippians 3:13

Prayer-meditation: Father, when understanding eludes me as I struggle to find meaning in some of the circumstances of life, I am encouraged by Paul's statement here. Give me that adventurous faith that will move on ahead, trusting You to lead and ultimately to give understanding.

My prayer requests:	*God's answers:*

FEBRUARY SUMMARY

March 1

God's Word to me: And the Word was made flesh, and dwelt among us...

John 1:14

Prayer-meditation: Lord, Jesus, how I praise You for being willing to take the form of a servant, to be the Son of Man in true humanity. How grateful I am that You have walked every dusty, weary, lonesome, frightening trail of earthly life ahead of me. Otherwise, Lord, You could be for me only a figure in a stained-glass window or a spotless statue in a niche—inaccessible, unapproachable.

My prayer requests:	*God's answers:*

CHRIST'S HUMANITY

March 2

God's Word to me: . . . Christ Jesus, who . . . emptied Himself . . . being born in the likeness of men.

Philippians 2:5, 7 (RSV)

Prayer-meditation: Lord, until I grasp the truth that Your being true Son of Man was but a channel for the Father's power during Your days on earth, I am left only with trying to imitate You. Seeking to follow Your example, to be like You without Your Spirit inside me, would be like a candle trying to imitate the sun.

As You emptied Yourself for the Father's indwelling, I would now empty myself for Your Spirit's indwelling.

My prayer requests:	*God's answers:*

March 3

God's Word to me: Great indeed . . . is the mystery of our religion: He [Jesus] was manifested in the flesh . . .

1 Timothy 3:16 (RSV)

Prayer-meditation:
> May our prayer, O Christ, awaken all Thy human
> reminiscences . . .
>> PETER MARSHALL

Awesome indeed, O Lord, is the sharp reality of Your tabernacling in human flesh. You grew as all boys grow: helped in the carpenter shop, learned to fashion perfectly curved yokes for the oxen, knew what it was to be tired, to know hunger and thirst, to have aching muscles. You too felt hot tears running down Your cheeks. On the cross the nails being driven in were as agonizing to Your flesh as to any man's.

I praise You for being my Brother-Christ as well as my Lord.

My prayer requests: | *God's answers:*

March 4

God's Word to me: ... I assure you ... the Son is able to do nothing from Himself—of His own accord; but He is able to do only what He sees the Father doing.

John 5:19 (AMPLIFIED)

Prayer-meditation: Do we really believe Him? That of Himself, He was as helpless as we are to perform miracles? That His wonder-working power came only as the result of the Father in Him?

Lord, I see that unless I do believe You here, a promise like John 14:12 makes no sense. As the Father in You did the works, so You intend for the Holy Spirit in me to do the works. What a glorious plan!

My prayer requests:	*God's answers:*

March 5

God's Word to me: But I say to you, Love your enemies . . . Do not lay up for yourselves treasures on earth . . . do not be anxious about tomorrow . . . Judge not, that you be not judged.
Matthew 5:44; 6:19, 34; 7:1 (RSV)

Prayer-meditation: Lord Jesus, what an impossible ethic You have given us in the Sermon on the Mount! Even as these words of teaching first fell from your lips, You knew that the bravest human effort, the greatest will power would never come close to achieving this. Even then the cross loomed ahead, and beyond that, a glorious resurrection; and finally, the sending of Your Holy Spirit.

Now I understand: from the beginning You knew that this impossible ethic made no sense apart from the enabling power of Your Spirit inside me to live it out. For instance, when I cannot possibly love my enemy, You, inside me, can —and will. Praise You, Jesus, praise You!

My prayer requests:

God's answers:

March 6

God's Word to me: . . . He entered into a certain village: and a certain woman named Martha received Him into her house.

Luke 10:38

Prayer-meditation:
>   God gave all men all earth to love,
>   But since our hearts are small,
>   Ordained for each one spot should prove
>   Beloved over all.

RUDYARD KIPLING

Like all of us, the human Jesus had a favourite spot—the home of Mary, Martha, and Lazarus in the village of Bethany, only a hilly mile or two from Jerusalem.

Bethany marked the start of His triumphant entry into Jerusalem; it was from there that He ascended into heaven.

Knowing of His spot "beloved over all" draws us very close to Him. Our hearts understand!

My prayer requests:

God's answers:

March 7

God's Word to me: ... Your Father knows what you need before you ask Him.

Matthew 6:8 (RSV)

Prayer-meditation: Sometimes I have thought it selfish to pray about the petty details of everyday living. But the total stream of our lives is the sum of just such minutiae. And Jesus concerned Himself with those very things: people's health problems, securing the money for Peter's tax, a woman who had lost one coin, one little lost sheep, the contents of a little boy's lunch box so that a hungry crowd could be fed.

Father, this tremendous truth that You care about my life like that, seems too good to be true. I praise You that it is too good *not* to be true.

My prayer requests:

God's answers:

PRAYER FOR OTHERS

March 8

God's Word to me: But I have prayed for thee, that thy faith fail not ...

Luke 22:32
(Read also Luke 22:54–62)

Prayer-meditation: Lord, this morning, greatly concerned about _____ , I would pray for my friend. Suddenly, I see that the key to answered prayer for another is *my* faith that You do have a beautiful, joyous plan for this life, and that Your power can foil all of Satan's attempts to interfere with that plan. In praying for _____ , how wonderful that You lift my eyes from any appraisal of mine about _____ , to focus on *Your* strength and power.

My prayer requests:	*God's answers:*

March 9

God's Word to me: I desire then that in every place the men should pray ... Rejoice always, pray constantly ...
1 Timothy 2:8; 1 Thessalonians 5:16, 17 (RSV)

Prayer-meditation: In order to pray constantly, it is going to have to be in the daily routine: in the car when stopped by a red light; asking You for a parking place; just before I make that special telephone call; pausing right then to pray for a friend rather than just talking about his (her) needs; at the side of my sick friend; before each meal. So, Lord, help me to saturate my life with the lubricating oil of prayer.

My prayer requests:

God's answers:

March 10

God's Word to me: . . . God forbid that I should sin against the Lord in ceasing to pray for you . . .

1 Samuel 12:23
(Read also 1 Thessalonians 5:17)

Prayer-meditation: This verse startles me, Lord. I have stopped praying for a person in need because I got weary, or was annoyed at the lack of results, or simply because I forgot. I see now that You take our commitments to pray for others so seriously that to fail to pray is actually a sin of omission.

My prayer requests:	*God's answers:*

THE SACRIFICE OF PRAYER

March 11

God's Word to me: And in the morning, rising up a great while before day, He went out, and departed into a solitary place, and there prayed.

Mark 1:35

Prayer-meditation: Lord Jesus, every time I read this scripture I feel guilty because it is so hard to get up early in the morning. When I do rise early, desiring to have time with You, it takes so long to get my thoughts focused and receptive. Help me, Lord, to overcome wandering thoughts and the desire for sleep—and increase my love for You so much that eagerly I'll want to rise early for communion with You.

My prayer requests:	God's answers:

ASKING PRAYER
March 12

God's Word to me: So I tell you, whatever you pray for and ask, believe you have got it, and you shall have it.

Mark 11:24 (MOFFATT)

Prayer-meditation: Hope must be in the future tense. Faith —to be faith—must always be in the present tense. Only faith will forgive sins, or resist Satan, or heal. In the gospels we watch Jesus putting into practice the principle given us in Mark 11:24. Zacchaeus had spent his life in sin. Yet Jesus said, "*This* day is salvation come to this house" (Luke 19:9). The man at the pool of Bethesda had been a cripple for thirty-eight years. Yet Jesus told him to pick up his mat and walk *now* (John 5:8).

Lord, my prayer is, "Thy kingdom come for me in every area of my life *now*."

My prayer requests:

God's answers:

March 13

God's Word to me: And Jesus looking upon them saith, With men it is impossible, but not with God: for with God all things are possible.

Mark 10:27

Prayer-meditation: I love this promise, Lord, because it helps me see myself as I am. So often situations bewilder or overwhelm me; I almost feel defeated before I begin to think through possible solutions. Then I remember that You have walked this way before me. Alone I am weak, but You have promised me Your strength. Alone I can do nothing creative, but You can work all things out to the best for everyone concerned.

My prayer requests:	*God's answers:*

PRAYER FOR DISCERNMENT

March 14

God's Word to me: For false Christs and false prophets shall rise, and shall shew signs and wonders, to seduce, if it were possible, even the elect.

Mark 13:22

Prayer-meditation: I pray for discernment, Lord, to know a false prophet when I see one. Keep me from impulsive judgments of spiritual leaders when I disagree with any of them. But sound the warning bells inside me when You want me either to confront one with Your truth or simply to walk away.

My prayer requests:

God's answers:

March 15

God's Word to me: Wherefore He [Jesus] is able also to save them to the uttermost that come unto God by Him, seeing He ever liveth to make intercession for them.

Hebrews 7:25

Prayer-meditation: O risen and glorified Lord, how I praise You, that as great High Priest before the throne of the Father, You are my personal Advocate. *Your* prayers are always answered!

In the hour of trial, Jesus plead for me;
Lest by base denial, I depart from Thee:
When Thou seest me waver, With a look recall,
Nor for fear or favour, Suffer me to fall.

JAMES MONTGOMERY, 1834

My prayer requests:	*God's answers:*

March 16

God's Word to me: . . . ask, and ye shall receive . . . What would ye that I should do for you?

John 16:24; Mark 10:36

Prayer-meditation:
  "Praying is dangerous business."

PETER MARSHALL

I asked for patience, Lord, and You sent me the slowest cleaning woman I've ever had. I asked for love, and You sent a cross-grained relative to stay with us for a month. I asked for the gift of faith, and for a season You withdrew Your face from me, forcing me to walk in darkness, trusting You blindly.

What a sense of humour You have, Lord! Your message to me is: "From here on, my child, be sure you mean what you ask Me for."

My prayer requests: *God's answers:*

March 17

God's Word to me: . . . My heart rejoiceth in the Lord, mine horn is exalted in the Lord: my mouth is enlarged over mine enemies; because I rejoice in Thy salvation. There is none holy as the Lord; for there is none beside Thee: neither is there any rock like our God.

1 Samuel 2:1, 2 (Hannah's Song)

Prayer-meditation: By faith, O Holy Spirit, allow me to move beyond the surface appearance of my circumstance to touch the loving hand of my Heavenly Father. As I praise Him in everything, I know that He is showering me with the gift of Himself in whatever happens. I reach out to receive His lovingkindness.

My prayer requests:	*God's answers:*

March 18

God's Word to me: Repent therefore, and turn again . . . that times of refreshing may come from the presence of the Lord.

Acts 3:19 (RSV)
(*Read also John 7:37–39*)

Prayer-meditation: Lord, I have been going through a time of spiritual barrenness, of boredom and arid unhappiness. Pleasures once enjoyed have gone stale. I am often tense and ill-humoured. And You have seemed far away.

I repent of a certain enjoyment of this. Lord, how I need the cool, refreshing gift of the Holy Spirit in my life! I open my heart to receive Him.

My prayer requests: | *God's answers:*

THE SURRENDER OF THE WILL

March 19

God's Word to me: All we like sheep have gone astray; we have turned every one to his own way; and the Lord hath laid on Him the iniquity of us all.

Isaiah 53:6

Prayer-meditation: You are right, Lord. In my blind will I wanted to be an individual—not just one of the flock. Paradoxically, I simply conformed to the crowd. Lord, I surrender my wilfulness; give me Your willingness.

My prayer requests:	God's answers:

SPIRITUAL CLEANSING

March 20

God's Word to me: ... he that hath clean hands shall be stronger and stronger.

Job 17:9

Prayer-meditation: Lord, my hands have been in filth too many times. Today I stretch them out to You for a spiritual scrubbing. I want to bathe totally in Your Light so that every dirty place, both inside and out, is cleansed. Then when people look upon me, they will see me as You view me: cleansed completely through the blood of Jesus.

My prayer requests:	*God's answers:*

March 21

God's Word to me: But He answered her not a word . . .
Matthew 15:23

Prayer-meditation: Lord Jesus, recently when I turned to You inwardly to ask how I should reply to someone, Your answer was "not a word". Then You reminded me of Your silences in the gospels.

Lord, Your silences unsettle us, as they are meant to. How eloquently Your silence says, "You, my child, are out of order. Get back on the track."

My prayer requests:	*God's answers:*

March 22

God's Word to me: They are not of the world, even as I am not of the world.

John 17:16

Prayer-meditation: Father, I know that by the word of Jesus I am not of the world. But sometimes I find myself caught up in such a schedule of activities that my prayer closet is empty. Then my disposition becomes irritable, critical, self-centred and generally unhealthy.

Help me, Lord, to remember that my primary purpose is not to be involved in the world but to have unceasing fellowship with You, thereby becoming Your representative —Your hands and feet and voice in the world.

My prayer requests:	*God's answers:*

March 23

God's Word to me: Blessed be He that cometh in the name of the Lord: we have blessed You out of the house of the Lord.

Psalm 118:26

Prayer-meditation: To come in the nature of God, yet to dwell as man among men! Especially at this season, Jesus, we are acutely aware of the high cost of blessing and being blessed.

My prayer requests:	*God's answers:*

March 24

God's Word to me: He that committeth sin is of the devil; for the devil sinneth from the beginning. For this purpose the Son of God was manifested, that He might destroy the works of the devil.

1 John 3:8

Prayer-meditation: How great it is to know that Jesus has won the victory over Satan, that whenever we are attacked, oppressed, or tempted by the evil one, we too can win the victory by claiming the power of the name of Jesus.

My prayer requests:	*God's answers:*

March 25

God's Word to me: And when the chief priests and Pharisees had heard His parables, they perceived that He spake of them.

Matthew 21:45

Prayer-meditation: Jesus, even the priests and Pharisees were more perceptive than I have often been. I usually think of someone else Your teaching fits, not me. Realistically, Lord, Your word applies to me. Help me to absorb and utilize it.

My prayer requests:	God's answers:

HE FINISHES HIS WORK

March 26

God's Word to me: The Lord will perfect that which concerns me ... forsake not the works of Your own hands.

Psalm 138:8 (AMPLIFIED)
(*Read also Philippians 1:6*)

Prayer-meditation:

Give what You demand of me and then ask what You will.

ST. AUGUSTINE

My prayer requests:	*God's answers:*

March 27

God's Word to me: I have manifested Thy name unto the men which Thou gavest Me out of the world . . .

John 17:6

Prayer-meditation: How often, Jesus, I have quipped, "What's in a name anyway?" But it is obvious here that names are very important—for You speak of personifying the Name of God the Father to those who shared daily life with You.

That seems to mean that in the handling of all my domestic relationships, attitudes towards work, pleasure, and people —as well as worship—all should manifest God in me to others.

Come, Holy Spirit, infuse me anew!

My prayer requests: | *God's answers:*

March 28

God's Word to me: And now, O Father, glorify Thou Me with Thine own self with the glory which I had with Thee before the world was.

John 17:5

Prayer-meditation: It is here that I first began to realize the great cost to You, Jesus, in being born of a woman, in deliberately taking upon Yourself the limitations of finite man, in leaving Your heavenly glory to come to earth to be the door of reconciliation between man and God.

"Our God to earth come down!" How glorious! What cost!

My prayer requests:	*God's answers:*

March 29

God's Word to me: These words spake Jesus, and lifted up His eyes to heaven, and said, Father, the hour is come; glorify Thy Son, that Thy Son also may glorify Thee.

John 17:1

Prayer-meditation: What a contrast this Scripture presents to my life! Jesus knew that the "hour of the cross" had come. Yet He asked only for the Father's help in completing His sacrificial mission—the reason He had come to earth— that the Father would be glorified in the Son.

Lord, deliver me from looking for personal spiritual rewards. Lift my eyes to the larger horizon of Your Kingdom and Your glory.

My prayer requests:	*God's answers:*

CHRIST'S PASSION

March 30

God's Word to me: Then He took unto Him the twelve, and said unto them, Behold, we go up to Jerusalem, and all things that are written by the prophets concerning the Son of man shall be accomplished.

Luke 18:31

Prayer-meditation: What incredible courage! With all the agony of Gethsemane already in Your Spirit, You deliberately went forward. Help me to remember that, Lord, when I would flee from trouble.

My prayer requests:	*God's answers:*

March 31

God's Word to me: Greater love hath no man than this, that a man lay down his life for his friends.

John 15:13

Prayer-meditation: Lord, my life consists of my desires, my needs, my demands, my opinions. You are asking me to lay these aside, put them down on behalf of my family and friends. It's easier to do, Jesus, when Your love is in my heart. Give me your kind of life-giving love.

And when I am tempted to self-pity in my giving and serving, grant that I may hear Your words: "This is the greatest form of love and it pleases Me."

My prayer requests: | *God's answers:*

MARCH SUMMARY

April 1

God's Word to me: ... and the chief priests and the scribes sought how they might take Him by craft, and put Him to death. But they said, Not on the feast day, lest there be an uproar of the people.

Mark 14:1, 2

Prayer-meditation: Nothing more clearly shows Your total sovereignty, Father. The cunning of man could not move forward by one second Your timing of the sacrifice of Your Son. O God, give me such faith in Your overruling sovereignty that I am delivered from concern about the reactions of people. And create in me a holy awe that final power in heaven and on earth is still Yours.

My prayer requests:	*God's answers:*

JESUS, OUR PASCHAL SACRIFICE

April 2

God's Word to me: . . . but God chose what is foolish in the world to shame the wise, God chose what is weak in the world to shame the strong.

1 Corinthians 1:27 (RSV)

Prayer-meditation: For the Israelites across long centuries, a helpless lamb was commanded by God to be their sacrifice for sin. And so, in the fullness of time, a baby, lying in the crook of a woman's arm, was in reality God tabernacling with men through the tiny body. He, the Child, as helpless as the lamb, would become our paschal sacrifice in order to reign as King of Kings and Lord of Lords.

My prayer requests:

God's answers:

April 3

God's Word to me: And [Jesus] saith unto them, My soul is exceeding sorrowful unto death: tarry ye here, and watch . . . And when He returned, He found them asleep again . . . neither wist they what to answer Him.

Mark 14:34, 40

Prayer-meditation: Jesus, how often I have failed here. Because I could think of nothing to say in prayer, I have allowed my tired flesh to rule—sleeping instead of watching and waiting for You to speak to me. Strengthen my spirit, Lord, to rule my flesh.

My prayer requests:	*God's answers:*

April 4

God's Word to me: Then answered all the people, and said, His blood be on us, and on our children.

Matthew 27:25

Prayer-meditation: Lord, this scripture has always horrified me by its incredible truth. For I have sometimes been guilty of wilfully ignoring Your Lordship in my life. Jesus, break my strong will and strengthen me where I am weak.

My prayer requests:	*God's answers:*

April 5

God's Word to me: Elect according to the foreknowledge of God the Father, through sanctification of the Spirit, unto obedience and sprinkling of the blood of Jesus Christ . . .

1 Peter 1:2
(Read also Exodus 24:4-8; Hebrews 12:24)

Prayer-meditation: As the priests sprinkled the blood of the sacrificial lamb on the altar and on the people, so You have sprinkled me with the blood of Jesus! How awesome! Yet I find a well of joy within, knowing, Father, that You will keep me under the protection of His shed blood as I walk in obedience with You.

My prayer requests: | *God's answers:*

THE RESURRECTION

April 6

God's Word to me: ... why seek ye the living among the dead?
Luke 24:5

... death hath no more dominion over Him ... in that He liveth, He liveth unto God. Likewise reckon ye also yourselves to be dead indeed unto sin, but alive unto God ...

Romans 6:9–11

Prayer-meditation:
> Love's redeeming work is done, Alleluia!
> Fought the fight, the battle won, Alleluia!
> Vain the stone, the watch, the seal, Alleluia!
> Christ has burst the gates of hell, Alleluia!

CHARLES WESLEY

My prayer requests:	*God's answers:*

April 7

God's Word to me: Jesus saith unto her, Mary.

John 20:16
(Read also John 10:11–17)

Prayer-meditation: Jesus called her by name, and Mary knew Him even by the way He spoke her name! The surge of her emotions was such that she reached out to hug Him to herself. But even as the grave could not hold Him, neither could her love restrain Him. Instead, His love held her at full attention as she listened to His instructions and in immediate obedience went forth to fulfil them.

O Lord Jesus, help me to live in Your Spirit—not in my emotions. Let my love for You issue in obedience to You.

My prayer requests:	*God's answers:*

THE RESURRECTION

April 8

God's Word to me: And the graves were opened; and many bodies of the saints which slept arose.

Matthew 27:52

Prayer-meditation: Jesus, You had just divested Your humanity, but you had conquered death! "O grave where is thy victory, O death where is thy sting?" This scripture confirms to me, Lord, that if I "die in Christ" I will surely rise to reign with You.

My prayer requests:	*God's answers:*

THE SPRINGTIME OF RESURRECTION

April 9

God's Word to me: For, lo, the winter is past . . . The flowers appear on the earth; the time of the singing of birds is come . . .
Song of Solomon 2:11, 12

Prayer-meditation: Thank You, Father, for the steady renewal of life. During the long winter months when the limbs of trees are bare, I know that spring will come again, that sap will rise and fresh green leaves appear. Even so, thank You that I need not despair through days drab with seemingly unimportant tasks, through dark periods of waiting for prayers to be answered, through times when I am unable to feel Your presence. Praise You that Your life is always there. Praise You for spring!

My prayer requests:	*God's answers:*

THE RESURRECTION OF HOPE

April 10

God's Word to me: Blessed be the God and Father of our Lord Jesus Christ, which according to His abundant mercy hath begotten us again unto a lively hope by the resurrection of Jesus Christ from the dead.

1 Peter 1:3

Prayer-meditation: Father, Job said, "You, O Lord, destroy the hope of man" (Job 14:19). So many times I have felt bereft of all hope; in this I can relate to the disciples in the period between the crucifixion and resurrection of Jesus. So thank You, Father, for Your great mercy in restoring our hope through Jesus Christ, Whom no grave could contain.

My prayer requests:	*God's answers:*

April 11

God's Word to me: Knowing that He which raised up the Lord Jesus shall raise up us also by Jesus ...

2 Corinthians 4:14

Prayer-meditation: "Knowing" always implies the most intimate relationship when used in Your Scripture, Father. O Lord Jesus, it is my heart's desire to have with You this deep, intimate relationship wherein personality is secure and complete at the heart centre.

My prayer requests:	*God's answers:*

RESURRECTION APPEARANCES

April 12

God's Word to me: . . . Jesus saith to Simon Peter, Simon, son of Jonas . . .

John 21:15
(Read also Matthew 16:15–20)

Prayer-meditation: There had been a day when Jesus had called him "Peter". Why? Because it was symbolic of the confession Simon had made when God revealed to him that the "rock" foundation of our faith is that Jesus Christ is the Son of God. But now, in this post-resurrection appearance, Jesus reverted to the family name to ask: What is your relationship with Me now, Simon? Do you love Me more than your own life? Are you prepared to confess Me as Christ and as Lord? Will you be Peter—or Simon?

Lord, help me fully and unashamedly to live in the name You have given to me—Christian.

My prayer requests:

God's answers:

April 13

God's Word to me: And it shall be said in that day, Lo, this is our God; we have waited for Him, and He will save us: this is the Lord; we have waited for Him, we will be glad and rejoice in His salvation.

Isaiah 25:9

Prayer-meditation: O Lord, open our understanding that we will not be as those who heard or read the promise of Your coming, yet never believed. Help us really to rejoice in Your salvation which has become the salvation of all who truly believe You and confess, "Yes, Jesus is *my* Saviour."

My prayer requests:	*God's answers:*

April 14

God's Word to me: And ye now therefore have sorrow: but I will see you again, and your hearts shall rejoice, and your joy no man taketh from you.

John 16:22

Prayer-meditation: "Joy cometh in the morning." It's true, Lord! As I awaken to greet You with each new day, my heart springs with joy. As You impart Yourself to me, I find that circumstances of life can dim but never destroy the joy You have given me.

My prayer requests:	*God's answers:*

April 15

God's Word to me: To an inheritance incorruptible, and unde-filed, and that fadeth not away, reserved in heaven for you.

1 Peter 1:4

Prayer-meditation: "Joint-heirs with Christ" (Romans 8:17). Our future reservations have already been made in heaven! But we are joint heirs here too in facing opposition, persecution, unbelief! Lord, keep me mindful that as a joint heir with You, all the power of heaven is available to me here and now to keep that which You have won for me.

My prayer requests:	*God's answers:*

THE TRANSFIGURATION

April 16

God's Word to me: And [Jesus] was transfigured before them: and His face did shine as the sun, and His raiment was white as the light. And, behold, there appeared unto them Moses and Elijah talking with Him.

Matthew 17:2, 3

Prayer-meditation: Father, I want that joy in conversation that Jesus, Moses and Elijah shared with You. Give me that exciting quest of spirit that thrills in sharing Your fresh concepts and ideas, then putting them into practice.

My prayer requests: | *God's answers:*

April 17

God's Word to me: Then a voice came from heaven . . . The crowd standing by heard it and said that it had thundered.

John 12:28, 29 (RSV)
(Read also John 12:20–36)

Prayer-meditation: I am discovering, Lord, that in every answer to prayer, every modern miracle of guidance or healing or changed lives, You still always leave room for the unbelief of those who say, "Oh, only coincidence", or, "It's only thunder".

Thank You for alerting us to expect this stubborn unbelief (Luke 16:31) so that our faith will not be shaken nor our praise diminished by it.

My prayer requests:	*God's answers:*

April 18

God's Word to me: I can of mine own Self do nothing: as I hear, I judge: and My judgment is just . . .

John 5:30

Prayer-meditation: . . . "as I hear" . . . I must stop and really listen to You, Lord, then let my decision arise from what You say to me. Lord, I do want to follow You. Yet often I have excused my self-will by saying that Your will has not been clear. Now I make You Master of my life. Help me to-day to obey You unquestioningly and immediately, leaving the results to You.

My prayer requests:	*God's answers:*

April 19

God's Word to me: For we which live are alway delivered unto death for Jesus' sake, that the life also of Jesus might be made manifest in our mortal flesh.

2 Corinthians 4:11

Prayer-meditation: Lord, every time I become conscious of sin in me, I suffer "death". For I find with Paul that my spirit longs to be totally submissive unto You. Yet I am grieved to find sin still active within me. Lord, continue in me Your work of cleansing, that Your resurrection life will be the life manifested in me.

My prayer requests:

God's answers:

April 20

God's Word to me: Thou wilt keep him in perfect peace whose mind [imagination] is stayed on Thee.

Isaiah 26:3 (RSV)

Prayer-meditation: I know, Lord, that one of the places Satan gets to me is through my imagination. In every circumstance, he can present, "What if?" followed by negative pictures. I would now hand my imagination over to You, asking that You purify it, baptize it, possess it.

My prayer requests:	*God's answers:*

April 21

God's Word to me: Yea, before the day was, I am He; and there is none that can deliver out of My hand ...

Isaiah 43:13
(Read also John 10:28, 29)

Prayer-meditation: Thank You, O loving Father, for this wonderful promise! Here I find confidence that even when I am weak and faltering, because I have committed my life to You, no one—no evil power—can "pluck" me out of Your hand. You have accepted full responsibility for keeping me for Yourself.

My prayer requests:	God's answers:

April 22

God's Word to me: Sing to God, sing praises to His name: cast up a highway for Him who rides through the deserts; His name is the Lord, be in high spirits and glory before Him!

Psalm 68:4 (AMPLIFIED)

Prayer-meditation: It's spring, Lord. The earth is very beautiful, and my heart is singing. This morning I saw Your handiwork in the beauty of masses of rhododendron. What consummate artistry!

I heard Your voice in a child's bubbling laughter. I felt Your tender compassion as a baby robin fell out of the nest and had to be rescued.

Thank You for eyes to appreciate the beauty You have made, for a spirit to stand on tiptoe and worship You.

My prayer requests: | *God's answers:*

April 23

God's Word to me: . . . It is written, My house is the house of prayer: but ye have made it a den of thieves.

Luke 19:46

Prayer-meditation: Father, as I reflect on this Scripture I realize that I have often allowed the thieving thoughts of cares and concerns to rob both You and me of our time for precious dialogue. I commit all my thoughts to You that You may sift out the chaff and gather the grain.

My prayer requests: | *God's answers:*

BALANCE OF FAITH AND WORKS

April 24

God's Word to me: And seeing a fig tree afar off having leaves, He came, if haply He might find any thing thereon: and when He came to it, He found nothing but leaves; for the time of figs was not yet.

Mark 11:13

Prayer-meditation: Lord, as the leaves and fruit grow together on the fig tree, so may the fruit of Your Spirit be in me —a testimony of faith and works well balanced.

My prayer requests:	*God's answers:*

April 25

God's Word to me: . . . the joy of the Lord is your strength . . .
And all the people went their way to eat, and to drink . . . and to
make great mirth, because they had understood . . .

Nehemiah 8:10, 12

Prayer-meditation: Slow me down, Lord, and let me enjoy
your world today. I fear that I have been too deadly serious,
too intent, even too religious. I want to laugh, to take delight in a member of my family, to be romantic for a moment,
to have some fun! It will be a gift from You I'd like to enjoy
for the sheer pleasure of it.

My prayer requests: *God's answers:*

April 26

God's Word to me: . . . I saw also the Lord sitting upon a throne, high and lifted up, and His train filled the temple.

Isaiah 6:1
(Read also Isaiah 6:1–13)

Prayer-meditation: Isaiah, an ordinary businessman of his day, was in the temple, worshipping the Lord, as was his custom. God had a job to get done and He needed a dependable human being. God saw Isaiah's heart at worship and asked, "Whom shall I send?" Isaiah caught the vision and answered, "Here am I, send me."

O God, help me keep my heart fixed on Thee and be open to a vision of the heavenlies!

My prayer requests:	*God's answers:*

April 27

God's Word to me: . . . A sower went out to sow . . . some seeds fell by the roadside, and the birds came and ate them up.

Matthew 13:3, 4 (AMPLIFIED)
(Read also Matthew 13:3–8)

Prayer-meditation: Lord, I am overwhelmed with the extravagance of Your love! For like the sower in Your parable, You never looked back to see where the seed was falling. You knew that where it was received it would bear fruit of its own kind.

Thank You, Holy Spirit, for preparing my heart to receive the seeds of such a love.

My prayer requests:	*God's answers:*

April 28

God's Word to me: Sanctify them through Thy truth: Thy Word is truth.

John 17:17

Prayer-meditation: It is wonderful Lord, how a long season of frustration and doubt can suddenly be dispelled by Your Word. As You trim away the unimportant and the superfluous, I pray that You will supply Your perspective and bring Jesus clearly into view. In this way the answer to a troublesome situation will seem so simple!

Continue, Father, to purify my thoughts by feeding in Your truth so that my actions will flow out of simple obedience into sanctifying power and blessing for others.

My prayer requests:	*God's answers:*

April 29

God's Word to me: Who is this that darkeneth counsel by words without knowledge?

Job 38:2

Prayer-meditation:
Thy law, O God, is truth and Truth is Thyself. I behold how some things pass away that others may replace them, but Thou dost never depart.

ST. AUGUSTINE

My prayer requests:	*God's answers:*

THE KEEPING POWER OF HIS LOVE

April 30

God's Word to me: Who shall separate us from the love of Christ? Shall tribulation, or distress, or persecution, or famine, or nakedness, or peril, or sword?... No...

Romans 8:35, 37 (RSV)
(Read also Romans 8:7)

Prayer-meditation:
O Love that will not let me go...
GEORGE MATHESON

We have been captured by You, O Lord, and are held so tightly that nothing will be able to wrest us from Your hand.

Your love penetrates even the vast domains of life-threatening powers. I am glad that I am Yours!

My prayer requests:	*God's answers:*

APRIL SUMMARY

May 1

God's Word to me: Except ye . . . become as little children, ye shall not enter into the Kingdom of Heaven.

Matthew 18:3

Prayer-meditation:
Spiritual life is the life of a child . . . Certainty is the mark of the common-sense life; gracious uncertainty is the mark of the spiritual life . . . We are not uncertain of God; but uncertain of what He is going to do next . . . Thus life is full of spontaneous, joyful uncertainty and expectancy.

OSWALD CHAMBERS

My prayer requests:	*God's answers:*

May 2

God's Word to me: And I will bring the blind by a way that they knew not; I will lead them in paths that they have not known . . .
Isaiah 42:16

Prayer-meditation: Thank You, Lord, for the promise of an adventurous life when we follow Your guidance. I ask for the gift of courage and boldness to take the new marching orders You give me.

My prayer requests:	*God's answers:*

May 3

God's Word to me: Behold, I am doing a new thing; now it springs forth; do you not perceive and know it, and will you not give heed to it? I will even make a way in the wilderness and rivers in the desert.

Isaiah 43:19 (AMPLIFIED)

Prayer-meditation: Once our lives are planted in the grace of God, inevitably He is going to lead us out into new, untried paths, for that is the way of faith. That is the way of growth.

Lord, when I see a door closing behind me, let me not be fearful. Your promise is sure: You *will* open another door, making a way for me in what looks like an impossible wilderness. Thank You for the power that turns deserts into rivers of blessing.

My prayer requests:	*God's answers:*

May 4

God's Word to me: Jesus saith unto her, Said I not unto thee, that, if thou wouldest believe, thou shouldest see the glory of God?

John 11:40
(*Read also John 11:1–45*)

Prayer-meditation: Martha had confessed Him with her own mouth: "Thou art the Christ, the Son of God." But she had not been listening to His words when He then asked, "Believest thou this . . . whosoever liveth and believeth in Me shall never die?" Even Mary, who had sat at His feet, who had anointed His head, did not really hear Him.

Lord, help us to shut out all the opposition of learned responses so that when You speak to us, we will have ears to hear You.

My prayer requests:	*God's answers:*

May 5

God's Word to me: And there appeared to them Elijah with Moses; and they were talking with Jesus.

Mark 9:4 (RSV)
(Read also Mark 9:2–8)

Prayer-meditation: God wants to give us a vision to prepare us for the future. As Jesus gave Peter, James and John the privilege of listening to His conversation with Moses and Elijah, so God likes to share Himself with us. But like Peter, we are uncomfortable in the presence of the Almighty God, and we interrupt Him—robbing ourselves.

Father, my busy mind keeps darting ahead in every conversation. Help me to keep quiet that I may really hear the quiet voice of Jesus' Spirit within.

My prayer requests:

God's answers:

May 6

God's Word to me: ... not walking in craftiness ...
2 Corinthians 4:2

Prayer-meditation: Father, do I rightly understand this verse of scripture to mean not to approach every situation and opportunity with, "What's in it for me?"; or always manipulating people to my desired ends?

Lord, I pray for negotiators of labour unions, legislators, civil rights movements—for all who have responsibility to and for people—that they will not walk in craftiness, but walk in Your light.

My prayer requests:	*God's answers:*

May 7

God's Word to me: While I live will I praise the Lord: I will sing praises unto my God while I have any being.

Psalm 146:2

Prayer-meditation: Forgive me, Lord, when I am too eager for tomorrow to appreciate today. Even now I would still my busy mind, turn my face to You and let my praise ascend to You.

My prayer requests:	God's answers:

May 8

God's Word to me: Are not five sparrows sold for two pennies? And not one of them is forgotten before God . . . Fear not, you are of more value than many sparrows.

Luke 12:6, 7 (RSV)
(Read also Matthew 6:24–34)

Prayer-meditation:
> Said the robin to the sparrow, "I should really like to know
> Why these anxious human beings rush about and worry so."
> Said the sparrow to the robin, "Friend, I think that it must be
> That they have no heavenly Father such as cares for you and me."

ELIZABETH CHENEY

Lord, I am the one trying to be "spiritual", You are the practical One. I put my troubles for today into Your capable hands and trust You for tomorrow.

My prayer requests:	*God's answers:*

May 9

God's Word to me: Therefore shall ye lay up these My words in your heart and in your soul . . . And ye shall teach them your children, speaking of them when thou sittest in thine house . . . when thou walkest by the way . . . liest down, and when thou risest up.

Deuteronomy 11:18, 19
(Read also 1 Corinthians 3:10–15)

Prayer-meditation: You certainly give clear directives to parents, Lord. What a sobering thought that our parent-hood is part of our "works" that will go through the fire of Your judgment. Keep this imperative in the forefront of my thinking, Father, for as I obey You, I know that You will be sovereign Lord over my children. How they need You in these times, Lord! How we, their parents, need You!

My prayer requests: | *God's answers:*

May 10

God's Word to me: Now therefore hearken unto Me, O ye children: for blessed are they that keep My ways.

Proverbs 8:32

Prayer-meditation: Lord, thank You for the young people today whose hearts are set on You. Strengthen and empower them to withstand the ridicule that sometimes comes their way. And daily add to their joy in You. I praise You for Your contagious vitality that flows to them, as attractive to the young today as when, long ago, young fishermen left everything to follow You.

My prayer requests:	*God's answers:*

May 11

God's Word to me: Who can find a virtuous woman? for her price is far above rubies ... Strength and honour are her clothing ... and in her tongue is the law of kindness ... Her children arise up, and call her blessed ...

Proverbs 31:10, 25, 26, 28
(Read also Proverbs 31:10–31; John 19:25–27)

Prayer-meditation:

On this day, our Father, we would thank You for our mothers who gave us life, who surrounded us early and late with love and care, whose prayers on our behalf still cling around the Throne of Grace, a haunting perfume of love's petitions ...

We know that no sentimentality on this one day, no material gifts, can atone for our neglect during the rest of the year.

So in the days ahead, may our love speak to the hearts who know love best—by kindness, compassion, simple courtesy, daily thoughtfulness.

Bless my mother, Lord, with Your benediction.

PETER MARSHALL

My prayer requests:	*God's answers:*

May 12

God's Word to me: Delight yourself also in the Lord, and He will give you the desires and secret petitions of your heart.

Psalm 37:4 (AMPLIFIED)

Prayer-meditation: Lord, I do have a secret petition today, a deep desire of the heart. I ask that You lead our children to the marriage partners of Your choice and that you, Lord, overrule in these crucial decisions.

And wherever these future members of our family are now, I ask You to bless them, to lead them to know You as their Lord, to protect and to guide them. I praise You for the answer to this prayer out there in the future.

My prayer requests:	*God's answers:*

May 13

God's Word to me: ... they shall still bring forth fruit in old age; they shall be full of sap [of spiritual vitality] and rich in the verdure [of trust, love and contentment].

Psalm 92:14 (AMPLIFIED)

Prayer-meditation: What a beautiful ideal for the golden years, Lord! I think with gratitude of _____ and _____ in our church fellowship, and of my own parents in whom this promise is so abundantly fulfilled. And I praise You that bearing fruit is not a matter of age but of the infusion of spiritual vitality from Your Spirit.

My prayer requests:	*God's answers:*

ABORTION

May 14

God's Word to me: Jesus said, you shall not kill . . .

Matthew 19:18 (RSV)

Prayer-meditation: Lord, I would talk to You this morning about _____. She has a difficult decision to make. Will she follow hundreds of thousands of her sisters today and kill her unborn child by an abortion?

You alone can create life, Lord. We cannot. And all life is very precious to You. There stands Your immovable commandment that to kill Your creation is to sin against the Creator Himself.

Lord, give _____ Your inner buttressing to see that the way out is the way through. And show the rest of us how we can pray, what we can do to stop this slaughter of babies.

My prayer requests:

God's answers:

May 15

God's Word to me: Jesus saith unto her, Touch Me not; for I am not yet ascended to my Father.

John 20:17

Prayer-meditation: O Lord, keep this teaching in my heart for I would not be guilty of handling with familiarity that which is sacred. Through Jesus, I know that an audience with You, Father, can be warm and friendly. But help me always to keep the right perspective that You are "very God of very God".

My prayer requests:	*God's answers:*

May 16

God's Word to me: Take heed lest you forget the Lord your God
... who led you through the great and terrible wilderness ... that
He might humble you and test you, to do you good in the end.

Deuteronomy 8:11, 15, 16 (RSV)

Prayer-meditation: I am discovering, Father, that every life
you intend to use mightily in Your service has a wilderness
experience. The Israelites did. Jesus did (Luke 4:1–12). Saul
of Tarsus did (Galatians 1:15–18).

It is a time of struggle, of disappointment, of prayers
seemingly unanswered—such as a long illness, or being
forcibly separated from those we love, or a period of help-
lessness through unemployment.

Thank You, Father, that my wilderness is a time of
growth, of learning, of spiritual maturation. I could not
handle the land flowing with milk and honey without going
through this.

My prayer requests: | *God's answers:*

May 17

God's Word to me: Behold, the Lord your God has set the land before you; go up, take possession . . . do not fear or be dismayed.
Deuteronomy 1:21 (RSV)

Prayer-meditation: Your Word makes it clear, Father, that it was nothing but unbelief and disobedience that kept the Israelites wandering in the wilderness for 40 years. Therefore, how long I stay in my particular wilderness depends on me.

Thank You, Father, that believing Your promises, trusting You for the next step, relying on Your supply is the way out for me. I praise You that it is *always* Your will for us to enter the particular promised land that You have prepared for each of us.

My prayer requests: | *God's answers:*

May 18

God's Word to me: The Lord also will be a refuge for the oppressed, a refuge in times of trouble.

Psalm 9:9
(*Read also Matthew 23:37*)

Prayer-meditation:
    Rock of Ages, cleft for me,
    Let me hide myself in Thee.

AUGUSTUS M. TOPLADY

O Lord, Thou Guardian of my soul, walk before me
through the dark shadows to lead the way in the midst of
danger. Be a hiding place of safety for me.

Then shall my troubled spirit know comfort and rest, and
fear shall flee away. What security to be nestled in a crevice
of the Rock which You are!

My prayer requests:	*God's answers:*

May 19

God's Word to me: Take no part in the unfruitful works of darkness, but instead expose them.

Ephesians 5:11 (RSV)

Prayer-meditation: I do not consider myself to be a crusader, Lord. But I know that it is Your plan to use every disciple as a warrior against the forces of evil that surround us. Lord, I am willing to be used. But give me the gift of wisdom to know what evil works I am to expose, how to expose them and to whom. Then give me loving words that carry the cutting edge of Your truth.

My prayer requests:	*God's answers:*

THE POWER OF AGREEMENT

May 20

God's Word to me: Again I say to you, if two of you agree on earth about anything they ask, it will be done for them by My Father in heaven.

Matthew 18:19 (RSV)
(Read also Luke 8:41–56)

Prayer-meditation: We notice, Lord, that in the case of Jairus' daughter, You permitted only the girl's parents and Peter, James and John in the room. Jairus had already shown his faith by sending for the Master. You wanted only those in the room who agreed in faith.

This reminds us of our friend Virginia, who these days is having the power of faith-agreement proved over and over. She too is finding that especially in prayers for healing, it is better to exclude those who cannot "agree".

Thank You, Lord, for teaching us this powerful principle of answered prayer.

My prayer requests:	*God's answers:*

May 21

God's Word to me: . . . if two of you agree . . . For where two or three are gathered in My name, there am I in the midst of them.

Matthew 18:19, 20 (RSV)

Prayer-meditation: During the last week, Lord, You have been showing us another facet of the power of agreement between us Christians. When two or more of us "agree" lovingly, positively, clearly within the framework of Your will, then You have promised always to be present—and the prayer is answered.

But when such a group of believers "agrees" negatively— usually criticizing or gossiping or judging self-righteously— then instantly Your Presence is withdrawn, and the door is opened to Satan and his design.

This is a stark, hard lesson, Lord. Help me to be watchful, vigilant against any such negative agreement.

My prayer requests:	*God's answers:*

May 22

God's Word to me: And when I saw Him, I fell at His feet as dead. And He laid His right hand upon me, saying unto me, Fear not; I am the First and the Last.

Revelation 1:17

Prayer-meditation: Lord Jesus, how often I have longed to see You face to face! Yet this Scripture shows how clearly we see our unclean selves when Your light enters our mortal lives. Even after so many years, and experiencing so much persecution, John prostrated himself before You with as much awe and fear as at Your first resurrection.

My prayer requests:

God's answers:

May 23

God's Word to me: Ye are they which have continued with Me in my temptations.

Luke 22:28
(Read also Luke 22:14–30)

Prayer-meditation: Did you think temptations would end when you were baptized in His Holy Spirit? The devil left Jesus only for a season; his harassment of the Son of Man continued even to the cross. How then did Jesus live without sin? By staying in constant communication with His Father and obeying God's every instruction.

Take time to be holy, Speak oft' with thy Lord.
Abide in Him always and feed on His Word.
W. D. LONGSTAFF

Lord, as You have instructed us, let my life be lived in constant dialogue with You and surrender to You.

My prayer requests:	God's answers:

May 24

God's Word to me: And it came to pass in those days, that He went out into a mountain to pray, and continued all night in prayer to God.

Luke 6:12

Prayer-meditation: Jesus loved the out-of-doors: for early morning prayer; a hillside or lakeside for teaching; a boat pushed out from shore for a pulpit; the Garden of Gethsemane.

Lord, I too need the healing of nature to my spirit. The heavens do declare Your glory, the earth Your love. For the peace and hush of the forests, the vastness of the sea, the grandeur of the mountains, the delicate beauty of flowers, I praise You.

My prayer requests:	*God's answers:*

May 25

God's Word to me: Blessed be the Lord, Who bears our burdens and carries us day by day, even the God Who is our salvation.

Psalm 68:19 (AMPLIFIED)

Prayer-meditation: Lord Jesus, how I praise You that You came to earth to be our burden-bearer; that when I struggle along trying to carry my own burdens, I am actually usurping Your role.

How well You already know My present load, Lord. With joy, I roll these burdens on to Your shoulders, rejoicing that You are indeed my salvation.

My prayer requests: | *God's answers:*

May 26

God's Word to me: In the world ye shall have tribulation: but be of good cheer; I have overcome the world.

John 16:33

Prayer-meditation: Our Lord was always clear-eyed. In His last intimate talk with His apostles before His betrayal, He promised them—and us—troubles, problems, "tribulations". It must be so, simply because we are in the world where man's self-loving sin makes so much go awry.

But "cheer up", He assures us, "I will never leave you or forsake you. And I have put all this world of troubles under My feet."

My prayer requests: | *God's answers:*

May 27

God's Word to me: God is love . . . Love does not insist on its own way.

1 John 4:16; 1 Corinthians 13:5 (RSV)

Prayer-meditation: On the human level, one of love's most obvious characteristics is unselfishness. Since God is all love—is of the essence of love—can His love be of different calibre? The truth is that God is not only unselfish, He is selfless. His every thought, purpose and plan since the beginning of time have been for His children's welfare and happiness.

Father, I am ashamed that at times I have actually been afraid of You. Give me now faith in Your selfless love for me.

My prayer requests:	God's answers:

May 28

God's Word to me: I pray not for the world, but for them which Thou hast given Me; for they are Thine.

John 17:9

Prayer-meditation: Lord Jesus, here You are giving me a sorely needed insight about prayer: I have spent much more time talking with You about those persons who steadfastly reject You than I have about those who love You and are committed to You. How reassuring that You, Lord, never cease to pray for those of us whom the Father has given You. Help me also to remember my responsibility to hold the members of the Body in prayerful intercession.

My prayer requests:	*God's answers:*

May 29

God's Word to me: God is a Spirit . . . No one hath seen God at any time . . .

John 4:24; 1:18

Prayer-meditation: Then since God is a Spirit, the world around us is filled with His presence. To the extent to which the ego, the old man in us, is put to death, God as Spirit can fill our minds and bodies and live in us, literally making us new creatures.

What an exciting truth, Father! I know that the very air I breathe is full of Your Spirit. This morning I open the door of my mind, my heart, my body to You and invite You to come in!

My prayer requests:	*God's answers:*

May 30

God's Word to me: If any one sees his brother committing what is
not a mortal sin, he will ask, and God will give him life . . .

1 John 5:16 (RSV)
(*Read also 1 John 5:14–16*)

Prayer-meditation: Lord, I have needed this word on how
to pray about _____ who has been fleeing from You.
What amazing authority You have given us, Your people!
What a privilege that You bid me pray for _____, with the
knowledge that You will find the way to restore and forgive
and give life.

My prayer requests:	God's answers:

May 31

God's Word to me: . . . if I have all faith, so as to remove mountains, but have not love, I am nothing.

1 Corinthians 13:2 (RSV)

Prayer-meditation:
My heart an altar, and Thy love the flame.
GEORGE CROLY

Accompany me today, O Spirit invisible, in all my goings, but stay with me also when I am in my own home and among my kindred . . . Forbid that I should refuse to my own household the courtesy and politeness which I show strangers. Let charity today begin at home.
JOHN BAILLE

My prayer requests: *God's answers:*

MAY SUMMARY

June 1

God's Word to me: Therefore if any man be in Christ, he is a new creature: old things are passed away; behold, all things are becoming new.

2 Corinthians 5:17

Prayer-meditation: I know, Father, that I must come to You just as I am. But I also know that I dare not go away just as I came . . .

Where I am blind, give me sight.

Where I fail to hear Your voice, please do something about my deafness.

Even where I deliberately choose to do what I know is wrong,

You alone can change my divided will.

For Lord, I acknowledge my total dependence upon You.

PETER MARSHALL

My prayer requests:	*God's answers:*

June 2

God's Word to me: For Christ is not entered into the holy places made with hands . . . but into heaven itself, now to appear in the presence of God for us.

Hebrews 9:24

Prayer-meditation: Jesus Christ is my advocate who mediates for me personally. Lord, help me to provide You with an honest witness which You may use to present my case in the Supreme High Court of God.

My prayer requests:	*God's answers:*

June 3

God's Word to me: Who is gone into heaven, and is on the right hand of God; angels and authorities and powers being made subject unto Him.

1 Peter 3:22
(*Read also Hebrews 7:25–28*)

Prayer-meditation: Lord, help me to remember this Scripture and to stand rock-firm on it when I'm feeling wounded, confused, and oppressed.

My prayer requests:	*God's answers:*

June 4

God's Word to me: Thou hast ascended on high, Thou hast led captivity captive: Thou hast received gifts for men...
Psalm 68:18

Prayer-meditation: O Jesus, how precious are these words to me. Thank You, Lord, that among the gifts for men, You have redeemed me for ever from being the pawn of sin.

My prayer requests: | *God's answers:*

June 5

God's Word to me: For ye were sometimes darkness, but now are ye light in the Lord: walk as children of light.

Ephesians 5:8

Prayer-meditation: I want to be Your "child of the light", Lord, for there has been so much darkness in my life. I pray that the luminescence of Your Spirit will flood through me, cleansing and eradicating every unclean spot or stain so that my body can be a temple of Your Holy Spirit.

My prayer requests:	*God's answers:*

THE HARD HEART

June 6

God's Word to me: Wherefore as the Holy Ghost saith, Today if ye will hear His voice, harden not your hearts, as in the provocation, in the day of temptation in the wilderness.

Hebrews 3:7, 8

Prayer-meditation: Hardening of the heart, like hardening of the arteries, sometimes creeps up on us almost imperceptibly. It did with the Israelites through their much murmuring and complaining. Even after their miraculous exit from four hundred years of captivity, their praise to God was short-lived, and self-centred complaints soon hardened their hearts. A good warning to us, Lord.

My prayer requests:

God's answers:

June 7

God's Word to me: Now when they heard this, they were pricked in their heart, and said unto Peter and to the rest of the apostles, Men and brethren, what shall we do?

Acts 2:37

Prayer-meditation: Lord, so often I have tried fruitlessly to convince and convict others of wrongdoing. This must always be the work of Your Spirit alone. So, Holy Spirit of God, use my mouth to utter the words that will enable You to convict the hearts of men—even as You used Peter—that men may believe and not die.

My prayer requests:	*God's answers:*

June 8

God's Word to me: . . . as My Father hath sent Me, even so send I you.

John 20:21
(*Read also Matthew 10:5–8; Luke 10:2*)

Prayer-meditation: Lord Jesus, I see that the good news can never take the world for Christ unless every disciple takes his commission as a personal, daily responsibility. It is my feet, my hands, my voice You want to use. Show me to whom You want to send me today, and give me Your words —not mine—for that one.

My prayer requests:	*God's answers:*

June 9

God's Word to me: Acquaint now thyself with Him [God], and be at peace ...

Job 22:21
(*Read also Job 42:1–6, 10*)

Prayer-meditation: Father, I am ashamed that I take time for human friendship and neglect Your friendship. I seek now Scripture's answer to the most pertinent question in our world today: what is our God really like?

During this morning hour I would sit at Your feet, Lord Jesus, to acquaint myself with You, and in Your face to see the Father.

My prayer requests:	*God's answers:*

183

June 10

God's Word to me: [Love] beareth all things, believeth all things, hopeth all things, endureth all things.

1 Corinthians 13:7

Prayer-meditation: "Many waters cannot quench love, neither can the floods drown it" (Song of Solomon 8:7).

O Deliverer, when the overwhelming floods of despair threaten to overtake me, transfer me to the realm of supernatural love. Then the unquenchable fire of your love, caught up by faith, will triumph.

My prayer requests: | *God's answers:*

June 11

God's Word to me: The second [commandment] is this, You shall love your neighbour as yourself.

Mark 12:31 (RSV)

Prayer-meditation: Thank You, Lord, for helping me see that I cannot love my neighbour properly unless I first love myself. But help me to separate the kind of self-respect that comes from knowing I am a child of the King from the self-love which leads to selfish living and indifference to others.

My prayer requests:	*God's answers:*

June 12

God's Word to me: Behold, thou desirest truth in the inward being; therefore teach me wisdom in my secret heart. Fill me with
joy and gladness; let the bones which thou hast broken rejoice.

Psalm 51:6, 8 (RSV)

Prayer-meditation:

I want a principle within,
Of jealous, godly fear,
A sensibility of sin,
A pain to feel it near . . .
O may the least omission pain
My well instructed soul,
And drive me to the blood again,
Which makes the wounded whole.

CHARLES WESLEY

My prayer requests:	*God's answers:*

June 13

God's Word to me: Submitting yourselves one to another in the fear of God.

Ephesians 5:21

Prayer-meditation: "In honour, preferring one another." To seek always the highest good is the sovereign preference of God, in order to build together a life that will bear, in abundance, the fruit of the Holy Spirit.

Lord, I see this as Your plan for every marriage. Help _____ and me to make it our plan for our home.

My prayer requests:	*God's answers:*

June 14

God's Word to me: And, ye fathers, provoke not your children to wrath: but bring them up in the nurture and admonition of the Lord.

Ephesians 6:4

Prayer-meditation: Father, sometimes we despair about the way "the world" all around us drags our children down. We praise You for telling us how to overcome this: as we parents obediently instruct and nurture our children in your ways, and are living examples for You every day, then You will fulfil for each child that great promise—"when he is old, he will not depart from it" (Proverbs 22:6).

My prayer requests:	*God's answers:*

June 15

God's Word to me: And these words, which I command thee this day, shall be in thine heart: And thou shalt teach them diligently unto thy children, and shalt talk of them when thou sittest in thine house, and when thou walkest by the way, and when thou liest down, and when thou risest up.

Deuteronomy 6:6, 7

Prayer-meditation: God's ideal, as presented in His Word, is that every husband and father is to be prophet and priest for his own home. He is to be the instructor and living example for the children in obeying the commands of God and the teachings of Jesus, with the wife and mother as the co-partner in both roles.

Father, let neither selfishness in use of time, nor any feeling of unworthiness or ineptness be the excuse for shirking this top-priority parental duty.

My prayer requests: | *God's answers:*

June 16

God's Word to me: As arrows are in the hand of a mighty man;
so are children of the youth.

Psalm 127:4

Prayer-meditation: Father, now that You have opened the
spiritual eyes of _____, he sees how his former life has
warped his children's attitude towards all authority. Lord,
as You renew the mind of _____, give him wisdom in
handling his household with the authority You have dele-
gated to him.

My prayer requests:	God's answers:

June 17

God's Word to me: Put on the whole armour of God . . . besides all these, taking the shield of faith, with which you can quench all the flaming darts of the evil one.

Ephesians 6:11, 16 (RSV)

Prayer-meditation: Lord, I know from experience that evil cannot be vanquished by moral platitudes or ethical ideals. I need an act of will even more than of reason, and that is what You mean by "faith"; not faith in myself, but in You, Lord, making me sufficient for everything. Grant me then, this most important weapon which can become the core of our defence.

My prayer requests:	*God's answers:*

June 18

God's Word to me: Put on the whole armour of God . . . having shod your feet with the equipment of the gospel of peace.
Ephesians 6:11, 15 (RSV)

Prayer-meditation: I pondered this for some time, Lord, until I saw that to protect ourselves from attack we must first be aggressive evangelists. Equip me with the love and boldness I need as I remember that the objective of our warfare is the destruction of evil and the coming of the kingdom of peace (the kingdom of right relationships) into every area of my life.

My prayer requests:	*God's answers:*

June 19

God's Word to me: Put on the whole armour of God . . . having girded your loins with truth.

Ephesians 6:11, 14 (RSV)

Prayer-meditation: Lord, how marvellous to be encircled by Your truth—the only ultimate fortress for freedom in our sin-sick world (John 8:32). Thus equipped, we can stand against Satan, the father of lies. With his deceptions he seeks to weaken our faith in God's love for us and power to help us, and by sowing doubts and fear, make us yet more vulnerable to his attacks. Praise You that truth hurled in Satan's face, forces him to flee.

My prayer requests:	*God's answers:*

June 20

God's Word to me: Put on the whole armour of God . . . and take
. . . the sword of the Spirit, which is the Word of God.
Ephesians 6:11, 17 (RSV)

Prayer-meditation: The Word of God, like a sword, protects me from faith-destroyers. But since a good defence
needs a strong offence, the Word too can go on the attack,
cleanly separating truth from falsehood wherever it is encountered and discerning even unconscious motives and
intentions in those around me.

My prayer requests:	*God's answers:*

June 21

God's Word to me: Put on the whole armour of God ... And take the helmet of salvation ...

Ephesians 6:11, 17 (RSV)

Prayer-meditation: This word comes through strong and clear, Lord. My salvation is through Jesus Christ, and I can begin each day with a conscience washed clean through repentance. Freedom, joy and confidence can accompany me wherever I go. Like a protective helmet for my mind, salvation protects me from the barrage of accusations with which Satan would condemn me.

My prayer requests: *God's answers:*

PROTECTION

God's Word to me: Put on the whole armour of God . . . having put on the breastplate of righteousness . . .

Ephesians 6:11, 14 (RSV)

Prayer-meditation: Thank You for showing me that righteousness is an attitude of the heart, Lord. It means right standing with You because of the blood of Jesus. I need this breastplate to guard against the cynicism and sensuality of our times.

My prayer requests: | *God's answers:*

June 23

God's Word to me: A merry heart doeth good like a medicine . . .
Proverbs 17:22

Prayer-meditation: You have made the day, Lord, and it is beautiful. Help me to bring Your joy to every person I meet.

My prayer requests:	*God's answers:*

June 24

God's Word to me: But they that wait upon the Lord shall renew their strength; they shall mount up with wings as eagles; they shall run, and not be weary; and they shall walk, and not faint.

Isaiah 40:31

Prayer-meditation: Rather than wait, we so often take our lives into our own hands and wear ourselves out with ambition and strife. God's promise is that if we will wait on His timing, all the ingredients for accomplishment will be there: strength, perspective, vision.

O Lord, I want to redirect my energies and enter into a quiet, peaceful place in relationship to You. And wait.

My prayer requests:

God's answers:

June 25

God's Word to me: Thou [Jesus] hast loved righteousness, and hated iniquity . . .

Hebrews 1:9

Prayer-meditation:

"Read for yourselves in the gospels Jesus' references to the world and you will be persuaded that the stench of this world's sin was ever in His nostrils . . . For He felt Himself standing in a garden in which life's lovely things were becoming rank and decomposing. It was true then, as now, that lilies that fester are worse than weeds."

PETER MARSHALL

Lord, I give You permission to change my tastes, my desire-world, so that I too will love righteousness and hate life's spoilage.

My prayer requests:	*God's answers:*

June 26

God's Word to me: . . . speaking the truth in love, we are to grow up in every way into Him who is the Head, into Christ . . .

Ephesians 4:15 (RSV)

Prayer-meditation: Father, cleanse me from twisted thinking and deceptive ways so that I will come to love the truth and reflect it in my thoughts, in my actions and in my words. Give me the courage to speak the truth, the selflessness to relinquish concern about pleasing people. But let me speak truth *only* in love.

My prayer requests:	*God's answers:*

June 27

God's Word to me: But have renounced the hidden things of dishonesty . . .

2 Corinthians 4:2

Prayer-meditation: Lord, as Your light of understanding penetrates my unconscious, I am discovering how much "acceptance" of dishonesty has crept on me unawares. I have not always been vigilant against deception, in fact, have sometimes condoned it in others when I saw my own desires mirrored in them.

Thank You, Lord, for making it clear that it is only as I stand firmly for open honesty in my personal life that I shall be free to confront dishonesty wherever I find it.

My prayer requests:	God's answers:

June 28

God's Word to me: The disciple is not above his Master, nor the servant above his Lord.

Matthew 10:24

Prayer-meditation: The words "master" and "lord" are not customary to our modern, daily vocabulary. Yet even to-day's Christian will use them in reference to Jesus. Does that imply that we truly are ready to be servants to the people around us? Jesus was. Are we prepared to be criticized for doing God's will? Jesus was. Are we willing to be a friend without thought of reciprocation, or even when it is turned against us? Jesus was.

Lord Jesus, You and Your presence are the reward of life to me. Let my service to others be done graciously and lovingly as unto You, Master.

My prayer requests: | *God's answers:*

June 29

God's Word to me: ... this is a rebellious people ... which say to the seers, See not; and to the prophets, Prophesy not unto us right things, speak unto us smooth things, prophesy deceits.

Isaiah 30:9, 10

Prayer-meditation: Father, I find inside myself the same soil out of which comes rebellion, even being "stiff-necked", preferring to heed my own counsel rather than Your wisdom.

And all around me I hear false prophets promising material prosperity and problem-free lives to all who give lip service to Your name.

O Father, give me an aversion to smooth talk and deceits; instead give me a thirst for Your truth.

My prayer requests:	*God's answers:*

June 30

God's Word to me: Submit yourselves to every ordinance of man for the Lord's sake ... for the praise of them that do well.

1 Peter 2:13, 14

Prayer-meditation: Father, never before had I known that it is Your directive that we "praise them that do well". Yet I find numerous Scriptures in which Jesus gave praise to men who performed acts of kindness, prudence and obedience (Matthew 20:1–16; 25:14–23). And Paul did not neglect to praise those who were faithful and obedient to his teachings (1 Corinthians 11:1, 2; Philippians 4:1). Thank You, Lord, for pointing me towards honest praise when I see that it is due.

My prayer requests:

God's answers:

JUNE SUMMARY

July 1

God's Word to me: And God saw every thing that He had made, and, behold, it was very good.

Genesis 1:31

Prayer-meditation:

Creator Spirit . . . forbid that I should walk through Thy beautiful world with unseeing eyes:

Forbid that the lure of the market-place should ever entirely steal my heart away from the love of the open acres and the green trees . . .

Forbid that when all Thy creatures are greeting the morning with songs and shouts of joy, I alone should wear a dull and sullen face . . .

I praise Thee, Creator-God.

JOHN BAILLIE

My prayer requests:	*God's answers:*

July 2

God's Word to me: I am come a light into the world, that whosoever believeth on Me should not abide in darkness.

John 12:46

Prayer-meditation:

Our Heavenly Father, we thank Thee that we live in a world where light is in control and where darkness is but the absence of light. Help us to keep our eyes upon the sunshine and not upon the shadows, upon the reality of Thy Love and not upon the counterfeits of the Wilderness.

GLENN CLARK

My prayer requests:	God's answers:

July 3

God's Word to me: . . . but they have rejected Me [Jehovah] from being king over them.

1 Samuel 8:7 (RSV)
(Read also 1 Samuel 8:1–19)

Prayer-meditation: Father, the Scripture this morning tells me that the principle of absolute authority, whether of incapsuled community-sects or of nations, is neither Your will nor Your way. I see that democracy governed by assemblies of free men could have sprung *only* out of Christianity.

Father, help us to cherish our freedom in You and the freedom remaining in this nation as a prized gift directly from Your hands. Help us to struggle to maintain it, to vote for it, work for it, fight for it. Father, how grateful we are for freedom.

My prayer requests:

God's answers:

REPENTANCE FOR THE NATION

July 4

God's Word to me: If my people, which are called by My name, shall humble themselves, and pray, and seek My face, and turn from their wicked ways; then will I hear from heaven, and will forgive their sin, and will heal their land.

2 Chronicles 7:14

Prayer-meditation: Lord, my heart is grieved for our nation. I am deeply sorry for the lack of integrity in relationships —relationships between the people of this nation and You, and even relationships between individuals. Father, I earnestly repent of our many sins, lest some forget, or in their ignorant rebellion, fail to do so. Lift up the hearts of Your believers in this country in order that a healing of this land might begin. And show my family and me our part in this healing.

My prayer requests:	*God's answers:*

July 5

God's Word to me: He shall call upon Me, and I will answer him: I will be with him in trouble; I will deliver him, and honour him. With long life will I satisfy him, and shew him My salvation.

Psalm 91:15, 16
(Read also Genesis 12:1–3; 26:1–5)

Prayer-meditation: Father, it seems that You mean this for nations as well as for individuals. Abraham and Jacob, for instance, represented nations, and yet You instructed them to pray in this fashion. And You admonish us to pray for those in authority over us. Would it not be right to pray that Your Holy Spirit would so move in their hearts and wills that they might call upon You to fulfil this promise for the entire nation?

My prayer requests:	*God's answers:*

FALSE PEACE

God's Word to me: ... the prophets of Israel which prophesy concerning Jerusalem, and which see visions of peace for her, and there is no peace, saith the Lord God.

Ezekiel 13:16
(Read also Ezekiel 13:1–23)

Prayer-meditation: The vision God gave to Ezekiel told of the coming chastisement of Israel. Courageously, the prophet reported God's message as it was. Father, I see that we human beings are all alike. When Your message is given in honeyed words of reward for us, we listen gladly; otherwise, we want to turn away.

Give us the courage to face truth: that You are holy but also righteous; merciful but also just; that disobedience always results in separation from You.

My prayer requests:	*God's answers:*

July 7

God's Word to me: At the commandment of the Lord they rested in the tents, and at the commandment of the Lord they journeyed: they kept the charge of the Lord, at the commandment of the Lord by the hand of Moses.

Numbers 9:23

Prayer-meditation: When I read how You guided Moses and the Israelites across the desert by a cloud (Numbers 9:15–23), I can see, Lord, that obedience to You is the key to a happy life.

My prayer requests: *God's answers:*

July 8

God's Word to me: Commit thy way unto the Lord; trust also in Him; and He shall bring it to pass ... In all thy ways acknowledge Him, and He shall direct thy paths.

Psalm 37:5; Proverbs 3:6

Prayer-meditation:

Take, O Lord, and receive my entire liberty, my memory, my understanding, and my whole will. All that I am, all that I have, Thou hast given me, and I will give it back again to Thee to be disposed of according to Thy good pleasure. Give me only Thy love and Thy grace; with Thee I am rich enough, nor do I ask for ought besides.

ST. IGNATIUS LOYOLA

My prayer requests:	*God's answers:*

July 9

God's Word to me: The meek will He guide in judgment: and the meek will He teach His way.

Psalm 25:9

Prayer-meditation: Since meekness—teachability—is a pre-requisite for receiving Your guidance, Lord, show me how to be meek without being a doormat, how to be humble without being self-righteous.

My prayer requests:	*God's answers:*

July 10

God's Word to me: . . . I will make darkness light before them, and crooked things straight. These things will I do unto them, and not forsake them.

Isaiah 42:16

Prayer-meditation: I confess it, Lord, there are dark areas in my life I have not wanted to bring into the light. I see now that if I am to receive Your guidance, all must be laid out before You, nothing hidden.

My prayer requests:	*God's answers:*

July 11

God's Word to me: He maketh me to lie down in green pastures: he leadeth me beside the still waters.

Psalm 23:2

Prayer-meditation: _____ has been laid on a bed of sickness and is agonizing about duties not performed. Is it possible, Lord, that upon occasion You must "make" us to lie down in green pastures to get our attention? Enable us to see each temporarily closed door as Your leading towards the green pastures and the still waters of a listening ear and a receptive and obedient heart.

My prayer requests: *God's answers:*

July 12

God's Word to me: There is a way that seemeth right unto a man, but the end thereof are the ways of death.

Proverbs 16:25

Prayer-meditation: Father, this Scripture reminds me of the old Scottish ballad, "You take the high road and I'll take the low road, and I'll be in Scotland afore ye." Today there are so many who are preaching "short cuts" to heaven. But Your Word clearly teaches that we cannot use a "low" road to reach a "high" place for "No man cometh to the Father except by [Jesus] Me".

Lord, make Your Word to us both spirit and life, that discerning the true from the false, we will be able to bring others with us on the "high" road as we travel to the place You have prepared for us.

My prayer requests:	*God's answers:*

July 13

God's Word to me: ... Trust in Him [the Lord] and He will act.
Psalm 37:5 (RSV)

Prayer-meditation:
Forgive us that we talk too much and think too little.
Forgive us that we are so helpless without Thee and
yet are so unwilling to seek Thy help.

PETER MARSHALL

My prayer requests:	*God's answers:*

July 14

God's Word to me: And He said unto them in His doctrine, Beware of the scribes, which love to go in long clothing, and love salutations in the market-places.

Mark 12:38

Prayer-meditation: Father, Your word tells me that the fear of You is the beginning of wisdom. Help me, Lord, not to become infatuated with being "spiritual", exalting myself and displacing You from the throne of my life.

My prayer requests:	*God's answers:*

July 15

God's Word to me: For I say unto you, That except your righteousness shall exceed the righteousness of the scribes and Pharisees, ye shall in no case enter into the kingdom of heaven.

Matthew 5:20
(Read also Matthew 23:1–36)

Prayer-meditation: Lord, in the caustic, vehement harshness of Your words in today's reading, I hear no Jesus meek and mild—rather the wrath of Jehovah thundering from Mount Sinai.

I hear Your abhorrence of spiritual posturing; of constantly taking my spiritual pulse while neglecting the obvious needs of those around me; of counting myself too superspiritual to relax and enjoy children and laughter and good fellowship.

Thank You for Your realism, Lord: that as long as I am in this body, I shall never grow wings and will do well to remember my creaturehood; that You want my feet planted firmly on Your good earth.

My prayer requests:	*God's answers:*

July 16

God's Word to me: Well done, good and faithful servant; you have been faithful over a little, I will set you over much; enter into the joy of your Master.

Matthew 25:23 (RSV)
(Read also Matthew 25:14–30)

Prayer-meditation:
Teach me, O Lord, to do little things as though they were great, because of the majesty of Christ who does them in us and who lives our life; and to do the greatest things as though they were little and easy, because of His Omnipotence.

PASCAL

My prayer requests:	God's answers:

July 17

God's Word to me: If any one thinks he is religious, and does not bridle his tongue but deceives his heart, this man's religion is vain.
James 1:26 (RSV)
(Read also James 3:2–18)

Prayer-meditation: Lord, I see that the discipline of my tongue is one of Your priority disciplines. This day, keep me alert to those inner checks when I should be silent; to the bridle of Your Spirit when I would speak a destructive or divisive word.

My prayer requests:

God's answers:

THE TONGUE

July 18

God's Word to me: And the tongue is a fire, a world of iniquity ... full of deadly poison.

James 3:6, 8
(Read also 1 Corinthians 3:3–5, 16, 17)

Prayer-meditation: Lord, Your Word is teaching me that wrong use of the tongue can defile not only my body but also my family and Your Body—the church fellowship—as well. I dare to ask You to make me a catalyst in my church that together we may be alert to this truth, ever working towards love and unity and upbuilding rather than falling into fractiousness.

My prayer requests:	*God's answers:*

July 19

God's Word to me: But He [Jesus] turned, and said unto Peter, Get thee behind Me, Satan: thou art an offence unto Me ...

Matthew 16:23

Prayer- meditation: It is a revelation to me, Lord, that Satan can speak through Your own apostle, or members of my family, or through me towards ill-temper or divisiveness or any of the tempter's destructive designs. Open my eyes to this, Lord. Teach me about it—how to handle it—and set Your guard around me and my family this day.

My prayer requests:

God's answers:

July 20

God's Word to me: ... for by your words you will be justified, and by your words you will be condemned.

Matthew 12:37 (RSV)
(Read also James 1:6–8)

Prayer-meditation: Lord, I see it! So often I have prayed with faith for a gift or blessing or healing, then have proceeded to cancel out my prayer with words of doubt and unbelief. Your Spirit would bid me use *words* of faith to strengthen and buttress and build faith. Help me with this, Lord.

My prayer requests:　　　　　*God's answers:*

July 21

God's Word to me: In the secret of Your presence You hide them from the plots of men; You keep them secretly in Your pavilion from the strife of tongues.

Psalm 31:20 (AMPLIFIED)

Prayer-meditation: Father, I am under a strange kind of assault from misleading stories and twisted facts. I never before realized how Satan can use the gossiping tongues even of fellow Christians to cause strife and divide churches. Today, for this situation, I claim Your great promise of being hidden in Your secret pavilion and protected by Your own presence.

My prayer requests: *God's answers:*

July 22

God's Word to me: So through God you are no longer a slave but a son, and if a son then an heir.

Galatians 4:7 (RSV)

Prayer-meditation: I praise You, Father, for the freedom of choice to become a son and an heir rather than a slave of Satan's; that as we voluntarily hand over self-will, You give us back the personality that is uniquely ours. Thank You for delivering us from Satan's slavery that seeks to suck out our selfhood and make us into assembly-line puppets.

Out of the fullness of the Godhead, Lord, Your Life spills joyously over into my life. You, Lord, are always positive and creative, ever adding or multiplying, while Satan seeks to destroy and spoil by subtracting.

United to You, loving and adoring You, it is Your pleasure that I, as a child of the King, be distinctly myself. Who but You, Lord, could have thought of that!

My prayer requests:	*God's answers:*

July 23

God's Word to me: But the Lord answered and said unto her, Martha, Martha, thou art anxious and troubled about many things: but one thing is needful: for Mary hath chosen the good part, which shall not be taken away from her.

Luke 10:41, 42 (ASV)
(Read also John 11:20–30)

Prayer-meditation: Master, recently I have neglected talking with you in prayer and sitting at Your feet to listen, giving busyness and preoccupation with the pots and pans of life as my excuse.

I know now that You have been trying to get my attention through a series of minor mishaps as life has gone awry when I do not look to You.

Forgive me. Help me now, along with Mary, to choose "the good part"—the best dish.

My prayer requests:	God's answers:

July 24

God's Word to me: In returning and rest shall ye be saved; in quietness and in confidence shall be your strength . . .

Isaiah 30:15

Prayer-meditation:
>   Drop thy still dews of quietness,
>   Till all our strivings cease;
>   Take from our souls the strain and stress,
>   And let our ordered lives confess
>   The beauty of thy peace.

JOHN GREENLEAF WHITTIER

My prayer requests:	*God's answers:*

July 25

God's Word to me: Apart from me [Jesus] you can do nothing.
John 15:5 (RSV)
(Read also John 15:1–11)

Prayer-meditation: Lord, this seems a drastic statement until I remember that every breath, every heartbeat is dependent on You. Forgive me for times when, in a rebellious or an arrogant spirit, I have tried to make it on my own. Your truth is that the self-deception of such "independence" is an exercise in futility and a waste of my life.

My prayer requests:

God's answers:

July 26

God's Word to me: And He .. rebuked the wind, and said to the sea, "Peace! Be still!" And the wind ceased, and there was a great calm.

Mark 4:39 (RSV)

Prayer-meditation:
> Commit thou all that grieves thee into the faithful hands
> Of Him who never leaves thee, Who heaven and earth
>   commands;
> For He, the clouds' Director, Whom winds and seas
>   obey,
> Will be thy kind Protector and will prepare thy way.
>   PAULUS GERHARDT (1607–76)

Handle the storms of our lives, dear Jesus, as surely as You did that tumultuous sea long ago. Speak Your word, and peace and rest will surely follow.

My prayer requests: | *God's answers:*

July 27

God's Word to me: Though He slay me, yet will I trust in Him.
Job 13:15

Prayer-meditation: O Lord, You know my plight and my total discomfort in adversity. Use it now to purify my praise of You. I glorify You, not just for what You can do for me, but simply because You are good and Holy and are supremely worthy of receiving all glory and honour and praise. I accept Your loving presence even in the midst of real trouble and trust Your goodness, no matter the outcome.

My prayer requests:	*God's answers:*

July 28

God's Word to me: Beloved, think it not strange concerning the fiery trial which is to try you, as though some strange thing happened to you.

1 Peter 4:12

Prayer-meditation: Sometimes, Jesus, when I'm hurting, I think of it as retribution for my sin. But You were utterly obedient to our Father, and You suffered graciously. Grant that whether through sin or innocence, I too may suffer all trials graciously and rejoice in the learning experience it provides.

My prayer requests:	*God's answers:*

July 29

God's Word to me: I will delight myself in Thy statutes: I will not forget Thy word.

Psalm 119:16

Prayer-meditation: What joy and peace reign in me when I actively pursue this commitment. Even hurting is easier, and the burden of decisions is lighter.

My prayer requests:	*God's answers:*

July 30

God's Word to me: For He shall give His angels charge over thee, to keep thee in all thy ways.

Psalm 91:11

Prayer-meditation: This is a staggering statement, Lord—"to keep thee in all thy ways"! It's wonderful to realize that You have assigned angels, not only to help me in moments of need, but even when that need has arisen out of my rebellion to Your guidance. Lord, let Your angels effectively block me from any way contrary to Your perfect will for me.

My prayer requests:	*God's answers:*

July 31

God's Word to me: And ye shall be hated of all men for My name's sake: but he that shall endure unto the end, the same shall be saved.

Mark 13:13

Prayer-meditation: Enduring "unto the end" is more important to me, Lord, than indulging in hatred for wrongs received. As Your Light dispelled the darkness of this world, so let Your love in me dispel hatred in others.

My prayer requests: *God's answers:*

JULY SUMMARY

August 1

God's Word to me: I know that my Redeemer lives.

> *Job 19:25* (RSV)
> (*Read also Revelation 1:18*)

Prayer-meditation:
  Jesus my Redeemer lives!
  I, too, unto life must waken.

THE MORAVIAN TEXT

O Lord, may this truth erupt out of the smouldering miseries of our despairing lives with such force as to burn all other pitiable realities in its consuming fire. This clarion call to reality makes all else of no consequence. Praise Your name!

My prayer requests:	*God's answers:*

August 2

God's Word to me: The Lord . . . is longsuffering to us-ward, not willing that any should perish, but that all should come to repentance.

2 Peter 3:9

Prayer-meditation: I hold to this promise, Lord, for those close to me who are indifferent or who reject You completely. I pray for them that their closed minds will open to You; that their eyes will be opened to see how their wrongdoing is shutting out all the joys and gifts that Your love would give them; that Your loving patience will melt their cold hearts.

My prayer requests:	*God's answers:*

August 3

God's Word to me: For we wrestle not against flesh and blood, but against principalities, against powers, against the rulers of the darkness of this world, against spiritual wickedness in high places.

Ephesians 6:12

Prayer-meditation: O Lord, how I need Your whole armour for this kind of warfare. All the strength and ingenuity of my human strategy is as nothing. Give me discernment, Father, to know the enemy so that I may quickly appropriate Your defence.

My prayer requests:	*God's answers:*

August 4

God's Word to me: God is a Spirit; and they that worship Him must worship Him in spirit and in truth.

John 4:24

Prayer-meditation: Cares and worries weigh me down, Lord, and hide Your face from me. Lift my spirit with Your Presence, so that I may worship You with love and a joyful heart.

My prayer requests:	*God's answers:*

August 5

God's Word to me: . . . the angel of the Lord came upon him, and a light shined in the prison: and he smote Peter on the side, and raised him up, saying, Arise up quickly. And his chains fell off from his hands.

Acts 12:7

Prayer-meditation:

Long my imprisoned spirit lay,
    Fast bound in sin and nature's night:
Thine eye diffused a quickening ray,
    I woke, the dungeon flamed with light:
My chains fell off, my heart was free,
    I rose, went forth, and followed Thee.

CHARLES WESLEY, 1788

Thank You, Lord, for removing all condemnation and for clothing me in Your righteousness. I rejoice to be alive in You, my Living Head.

My prayer requests:	*God's answers:*

August 6

God's Word to me: Delight thyself also in the Lord; and He shall give thee the desires of thine heart.

Psalm 37:4

Prayer-meditation: Lord, You are dearer to me than a whole company of people; You are my Friend. I rejoice in the life we share together. But when You looked upon Adam You said it was not good that man should be alone, and You gave him Eve. Father, I too long for a human companion with whom to share dreams and meaningful experiences. I entrust this desire to You.

My prayer requests:	*God's answers:*

August 7

God's Word to me: A little that a righteous man hath is better than the riches of many wicked.

Psalm 37:16

Prayer-meditation: I watched her enter the room. Perhaps about fifty, I thought. Attractively groomed, colour-streaked hair framed her suntanned face. Her expensive clothing and her trim figure belied her years. But it was her utter loneliness that caught at my heart. From her nervous chatter I glimpsed in the background a husband, a child; yet her life seemed strangely empty, devoid of purpose.

O Jesus, I pray that she will meet You.

My prayer requests: | *God's answers:*

August 8

God's Word to me: Then Jesus called His disciples unto Him, and said, I have compassion on the multitude, because they continue with Me now three days, and have nothing to eat ...

Matthew 15:32

Prayer-meditation: Father, we are a hungry people. We try to satisfy our need with indulgence in food and drink; with constant reading for knowledge; with sexual excesses. But we are still hungry.

Lord, I would be as those who fed only upon Your word for three days and quenched the thirst of their spirits with Your presence.

My prayer requests:	*God's answers:*

August 9

God's Word to me: For we do not have a High Priest Who is unable to . . . have a fellow feeling with our weaknesses and . . . assaults of temptation, but One Who has been tempted in every respect as we are, yet without sinning.

Hebrews 4:15 (AMPLIFIED)

Prayer-meditation: Temptation is a test by an alien power of an individual's spiritual possessions. Does not this explain the temptations of Jesus? And does it not also explain our temptations as "joint heirs with Christ" in the Kingdom of God? Had we not, through being "born anew of the Spirit" received into ourselves the very Spirit of God, Satan would have no interest in us at all. He is after the possession God has invested in us, that is, the indwelling Christ.

Lord, how grateful I am that Your indwelling Spirit is a bulwark against all the temptations of Satan.

My prayer requests:	God's answers:

August 10

God's Word to me: Yet in this thing ye did not believe the Lord . . .
Deuteronomy 1:32

Prayer-meditation: Keep us, O God, from the temptation of dividing Your commandments into great and small according to our own blind estimate, thus disobeying You by leaning to our own understanding (Proverbs 3:5).

My prayer requests:	*God's answers:*

August 11

God's Word to me: Thou shalt have no other gods before me.
Exodus 20:3

Prayer-meditation: God—Supreme Being, Sovereign—in control of all creation; Holy Spirit, at any moment, in any place—with any person, when I may be tempted to allow something or someone to usurp Your position in my life—alert me, that I may not sin. I would bow only to You—Father, Son and Holy Spirit.

My prayer requests:	God's answers:

August 12

God's Word to me: Thou shalt not make unto thee any graven image . . . for I the Lord thy God am a jealous God.

Exodus 20:4, 5

Prayer-meditation: Lord, I've usually thought this referred to carved objects—material objects. But sometimes *I* have tried to refashion myself and others instead of allowing You to do Your own work, conforming us all to Your image. I know You are jealous of Your position as God in our lives. I take my hands off. Help me, Lord, to give You freedom to make and remake as You will.

My prayer requests:	*God's answers:*

August 13

God's Word to me: Thou shalt not take the name of the Lord thy God in vain.

Exodus 20:7

Prayer-meditation: Forgive me for all the times I have used Your name irreverently, Lord. Forgive me for the times when I have remained quiet while hearing others curse in Your name. Give me wisdom and courage to handle such situations as Jesus would.

My prayer requests:	*God's answers:*

THE COMMANDMENTS

August 14

God's Word to me: Remember the sabbath day, to keep it holy.
Exodus 20:8

Prayer-meditation: How I have failed You here! I go to church, Lord, but during the rest of the day I do little to keep out of the blare and noise and confusion of the world. Recognizing that You have made the Sabbath a day of rest for my benefit, I would seek to be re-created in it and to keep it a Holy Day unto You.

My prayer requests:

God's answers:

August 15

God's Word to me: Honour thy father and thy mother: that thy days may be long upon the land which the Lord thy God giveth thee.

Exodus 20:12

Prayer-meditation: Your great promise attached to this commandment is often missed, Father. I praise You that, as in obedience, we honour our parents, Your gift is the reward of a long, full life on this earth to enjoy the human family You have given us.

My prayer requests: *God's answers:*

August 16

God's Word to me: Thou shalt not kill.

Exodus 20:13

Prayer-meditation: This Scripture invokes memories of wars that have occurred in my lifetime and especially of the conflict in Vietnam. Many of us supported a war that killed innocent people. Forgive us for our arrogance, Lord, and forgive me for a hard-hearted attitude towards a strange land and a strange people.

My prayer requests:	*God's answers:*

August 17

God's Word to me: Thou shalt not commit adultery.

Exodus 20:14

Prayer-meditation: O Lord, the lust of Sodom seems pale in the face of the degeneration of people today. We have all violated this command in either thought or deed and are in need of Your forgiveness. Today, Father, I pray that You will deliver from adulterous relationships, _____ and convince them of their real need of You.

My prayer requests:	God's answers:

THE COMMANDMENTS

August 18

God's Word to me: Thou shalt not steal.

Exodus 20:15

Prayer-meditation: Lord, we can be so self-righteous and yet so phony about stealing. We do not take money from a man with a gun; we do it through deceit. We do not steal a friend's car; we rob him of his time and honour and peace of mind. We increase our income by lying to employers and the government and call it being smart. Forgive us our hypocrisy, Lord.

My prayer requests: | *God's answers:*

August 19

God's Word to me: Thou shalt not bear false witness against thy neighbour.

Exodus 20:16

Prayer-meditation: Forgive me, Lord, for the times I've exaggerated a story about other people as a joke, or allowed a misconception to go by unchecked in order to build myself up at others' expense. Sometimes my secret intent has been to hurt someone purposely. Check my mind, stop my tongue whenever this temptation arises, and grant me the grace, if need be, to go back and correct the lies I have spread.

My prayer requests:	*God's answers:*

THE COMMANDMENTS

August 20

God's Word to me: Thou shalt not covet thy neighbour's house ... thy neighbour's wife ... nor anything that is thy neighbour's.
Exodus 20:17

Prayer-meditation: Lord, sometimes I find the focus of my attention is on envying what my neighbours and friends have. Cleanse me of any ardent covetous desire of another's possessions. Heal me of every obsessive desire for anything except to serve You with all my heart.

My prayer requests:	God's answers:

August 21

God's Word to me: And this is the judgment, that the light has come into the world, and men loved [preferred] darkness rather than light ...

John 3:19 (RSV)

Prayer-meditation:

God nowhere holds a man responsible for having the heredity of sin. But if when I realize Jesus Christ came to deliver me from it, I refuse to let Him do so, from that moment I begin to get the seal of damnation.

OSWALD CHAMBERS

Lord Jesus, give me a love of the light, a loathing of the darkness.

My prayer requests:

God's answers:

LOVE AND FORGIVENESS

August 22

God's Word to me: "If you love those who love you, what credit is that to you? Even 'sinners' love those who love them."

Luke 6:32 (NIV)

Prayer-meditation: Thank You, Lord, for showing me that I tend to make a tight little island of myself, my family and friends. Help me to spread my love to those in need, to those who do not ordinarily attract me.

My prayer requests:	*God's answers:*

August 23

God's Word to me: A soft answer turneth away wrath: but griev-
ous words stir up anger. The tongue of the wise useth knowledge
aright: but the mouth of fools poureth out foolishness.

Proverbs 15:1, 2

Prayer-meditation: Father, in the light of Your Word we
certainly have a lot of unwise people in the world. So few
are working for reconciliation among men and nations; so
many are speaking and acting in violence. Father, help us
really to listen to each other with respect for differences; and
then to listen to You before we make our answer, that Your
oil of true peace will be poured forth.

My prayer requests:	*God's answers:*

August 24

God's Word to me: And when ye stand praying, forgive, if ye have aught against any . . . But if ye do not forgive, neither will your Father which is in heaven forgive your trespasses.

Mark 11:25, 26

Prayer-meditation: Jesus, it is with shame that I face You and confess how difficult I find this teaching. It is so humiliating to admit error. Yet I dare not gamble with my salvation which You purchased by such forgiveness—at the cost of Your life.

My prayer requests:

God's answers:

August 25

God's Word to me: ... You shall love your neighbour as yourself.
Mark 12:31 (RSV)

Prayer-meditation: Because You are all love, Father, You will not tolerate any unforgiveness or hardness in me towards anyone. You command me to forgive, regardless of who is to blame. Thank You for the little parable You gave me this morning: The air around us is full of electricity, but it cannot be harnessed to work for us unless it is grounded. Similarly, the universe is full of Your power, Father. But that power cannot become operative to transform lives and answer prayer without Your ground wire—love of person to person. So, Father, in my will I let go of my resentment against _____ to let Your love become the ground wire for power in this life.

My prayer requests:	*God's answers:*

THE PEACEMAKERS

August 26

God's Word to me: Blessed are the peacemakers, for they shall be called sons of God.

Matthew 5:9 (RSV)

Prayer-meditation:
    Lord, make me an instrument of Your peace.
    Where there is hatred, let me sow love;
    Where there is injury, pardon;
    Where there is doubt, faith;
    Where there is despair, hope;
    Where there is darkness, light;
    And where there is sadness, joy
                ST. FRANCIS OF ASSISI

My prayer requests:	*God's answers:*

August 27

God's Word to me: Where there is no vision, the people perish.
Proverbs 29:18

Prayer-meditation: American Missionary Mark Buntain had a vision of Jesus walking the streets of Calcutta, leaning down to one after another of the pathetic, disease-ridden, starving persons who, having no homes, live and die in the street. With that vision before him, young Mark went to Calcutta. Christ, indwelling him, has given substance to the vision in the form of a hospital, a school, vocational opportunities—and greatest of all—*life* where there was death.

Help me, Lord, to catch Your vision for others and abandon myself to be Your hands, Your feet, Your voice in giving substance to that vision.

My prayer requests:

God's answers:

THE OPPORTUNITY IN EXTREMITY

August 28

God's Word to me: As we have therefore opportunity, let us do good unto all men ...

Galatians 6:10

Prayer-meditation: Remind me that in the worst situation and with the most unlikely person, there is a hidden opportunity. When the moment comes, nudge me, Lord, and reveal to me the good word or the good gift to be given.

My prayer requests: *God's answers:*

August 29

God's Word to me: . . . it is the Spirit that quickeneth; the flesh profiteth nothing; the words that I speak unto you, they are Spirit, and they are Life.

John 6:63

Prayer-meditation: Since I have asked before beginning that Your Word come alive to me during the reading, what a difference it has made, Lord, to the reading of Scripture! When I read the Bible because it was "something I should do", it was of no profit to me. Now Your Holy Spirit gives me such insights that I find it an exciting and exhilarating experience, lasting long after I have closed the Book.

My prayer requests:	*God's answers:*

INNER BEAUTY

God's Word to me: Let not yours be the outward adorning with braiding of hair, decoration of gold, and wearing of fine clothing, but let it be the hidden person of the heart with the imperishable jewel of a gentle and quiet spirit, which in God's sight is very precious.

1 Peter 3:3, 4 (RSV)

Prayer-meditation: By the message of her character (Monica, Augustine's mother), won her pagan husband to Christ whereby God made "her beautiful to him, reverently lovable, and wonderful" (St. Augustine's *Confessions*).

It is the hidden man, the heart, O Lord, who matters to You. And yet my outer appearance is a reflection of my inner man. Let me take stock: is my appearance a commendation for Christ?

My prayer requests:	God's answers:

August 31

God's Word to me: In Thy presence is fullness of joy, at Thy right hand there are pleasures for evermore.

Psalm 16:11
(Read also Isaiah 55:8–13)

Prayer-meditation: Joy looking out of the Christian's eyes is one of the signs that the King is in residence. Similarly, in prayer, joy is a sign of the Father's approval.

I ask Your forgiveness, Lord, that my joylessness is often such a poor advertisement of Your Kingdom. I ask now for Your gift of joy.

My prayer requests: | *God's answers:*

AUGUST SUMMARY

September 1

God's Word to me: And we labour, working with our own hands.
1 Corinthians 4:12 (RSV)
(*Read also Ephesians 6:5–12*)

Prayer-meditation: Father, Your blessing has always been on honest toil: from the first man Adam, whom You bade "tend the garden", to Jesus Himself, who must have mended the flat roofs of Nazareth and lovingly fixed toys for the village children, to Paul, who earned his own way by stitching sails and tents.

Father, let me use my work today as a worthy sacrament offered up to You.

My prayer requests: | *God's answers:*

September 2

God's Word to me: Whatever your task, work heartily, as serving the Lord and not men ...

Colossians 3:23 (RSV)

Prayer-meditation:

We look for visions from heaven, for earthquakes and thunders of God's power . . . and we never dream that all the time God is in the commonplace things around us. If we will do the duty that lies nearest, we shall see Him ...

OSWALD CHAMBERS

I saw your beauty, Lord, in the soapsuds-rainbow of my dishwater. I heard Your voice in a child's laugh. I saw You in the courtesy of the driver who motioned me into his place in line, and in the compassionate heart of a friend. Praise You, Lord!

My prayer requests:	*God's answers:*

September 3

God's Word to me: Do not love the world or the things in the world. If any one loves the world, love for the Father is not in him.

1 John 2:15 (RSV)
(Read also Mark 8:36)

Prayer-meditation: Lord, I have felt deadness encroaching upon my spirit when I have sought pleasures for their own sake. Self-gratification and self-indulgence leave me feeling empty, and yet I am tempted to seek the gain this world offers. In those moments, remove my blinkers so I will see these temptations as shoddy substitutes for the inner riches Your way provides. May Your love be found in me.

My prayer requests:

God's answers:

MONEY AND MATERIALISM

September 4

God's Word to me: Lay not up for yourselves treasures upon earth, where moth and rust doth corrupt, and where thieves break through and steal. But lay up for yourselves treasures in heaven...

Matthew 6:19, 20
(Read also Luke 18:18–27)

Prayer-meditation:

Lord, our hearts are hungry, as are the hearts of people everywhere. Save us from thinking, even for a moment, that we can feed our souls on things. Save us from the vain delusion that the piling up of wealth or comforts can satisfy.

PETER MARSHALL

My prayer requests:

God's answers:

September 5

God's Word to me: For the love of money is the root of all evil.
1 Timothy 6:10

Prayer-meditation: Thank You, Lord, for this reminder. In a world where money dominates nearly every area of our lives—and even the lives of most of our churches—through an act of my will I now separate my real needs involving money from my love of money itself and from any greedy desires. Show me, Lord, how to apply this, and give me the courage to act on it.

My prayer requests:	*God's answers:*

September 6

God's Word to me: Your gold and silver is cankered; and the rust of them shall be a witness against you . . . Ye have heaped treasure together for the last days.

James 5:3

Prayer-meditation: One thing is certain, Lord, we cannot take our earthly treasures with us at the end of life. How would You have us handle our possessions as we prepare for the last days? What will we need? What should we get rid of? We know not when You will return, Lord Jesus, but our heart's desire is to be ready.

My prayer requests:	*God's answers:*

September 7

God's Word to me: Bring the full tithes into the storehouse, that there may be food in My house; and thereby put Me to the test, says the Lord of hosts, if I will not open the windows of heaven for you and pour down for you an overflowing blessing.

Malachi 3:10 (RSV)

Prayer-meditation: What an exciting challenge to a decision of faith this is, Lord. Men in every century have proved in their own experience that we can never outgive God. I praise You for those windows of heaven spilling out blessing!

My prayer requests:

God's answers:

MONEY AND MATERIALISM

September 8

God's Word to me: Silver and gold have I none; but such as I have give I thee: In the name of Jesus Christ of Nazareth rise up and walk.

Acts 3:6

Prayer-meditation: What a glorious promise! My wealth is in You, Lord. The more I give away, the more You fill me with Your love, Your joy, Your supply for my needs.

My prayer requests:

God's answers:

September 9

God's Word to me: . . . when you give to the needy, do not let your left hand know what your right hand is doing, so that your giving may be in secret.

Matthew 6:3, 4 (NIV)

Prayer-meditation: You know, Lord, most of us like to be appreciated for our gifts. There are ways to give anonymously; I pledge to seek them out and so to experience in my life the blessings You have promised from secrecy.

My prayer requests:

God's answers:

BLOCKS TO ANSWERED PRAYER

September 10

God's Word to me: . . . your sins have hid His face from you, that He will not hear.

Isaiah 59:2

Prayer-meditation: Father, thank You for the lesson You taught me recently. After waiting a long, long time for a prayer to be answered, I was alerted to search my heart for any sin hiding Your face and blocking the answer. I found some resentment still there against two individuals. Alert all of us to the sins that hide Your face and defeat our prayers.

My prayer requests:	*God's answers:*

September 11

God's Word to me: And I beheld . . . in the midst of the throne . . .
stood a Lamb as it had been slain . . .

Revelation 5:6

Prayer-meditation:
>   Let earth and heaven agree,
>   Angels and men be joined,
>   To celebrate with me
>   The Saviour of mankind;
>   To adore the all-atoning Lamb,
>   And bless the sound of Jesus' name.
>   O for a trumpet voice,
>   On all the world to call!
>   To bid their hearts rejoice
>   In Him who died for all;
>   For all my Lord was crucified,
>   For all, for all my Saviour died.

CHARLES WESLEY, 1788

My prayer requests:

God's answers:

REPENTANCE

September 12

God's Word to me: And God saw their works, that they turned from their evil way; and God revoked His sentence of evil that He had said that He would do to them . . . for He was comforted . . . concerning them.

Jonah 3:10 (AMPLIFIED)

Prayer-meditation: God so longs to give blessings to His children. But when we are wilfully disobedient, justly He corrects us. As He sent Jonah to call the Ninevites to repentance, so He sends His Holy Spirit to warn us. As we repent and turn again to Him, God is merciful to forgive, always generous to restore His blessing upon us.

Lord, let my heart be as grateful and my spirit rejoice as much for the mercy You show towards another, as for Your gracious, overflowing mercy to me.

My prayer requests:	God's answers:

LORD, DISCIPLINE MY THOUGHTS

September 13

God's Word to me: . . . whatsoever things are true, whatsoever things are honourable, whatsoever things are just, whatsoever things are pure, whatsoever things are lovely, whatsoever things are of good report; if there be any virtue, and if there be any praise, think [calculate] on these things.

Philippians 4:8 (ASV)
(Read also Philippians 4:7–9)

Prayer-meditation: "These things" are qualities of life known to us only as we live them out.

Lord, my mind is undisciplined and battered with suggestions from many sources to commit myself to other things—things which will not bring peace with God. Help me to commit myself to Your set of principles, to Your standard of action, that Your own character might be formed in me.

My prayer requests:

God's answers:

PRAYER FOR CHILDREN

September 14

God's Word to me: Then were there brought unto Him little children, that He should put His hands on them, and pray: and the disciples rebuked them.

Matthew 19:13

Prayer-meditation: My heart was burdened for children this morning, Lord, as I thought of the pollution and false teachings pouring into their minds from television, from motion pictures and pornographic literature, even through the secularism and godlessness of our schools. I would pray for all children, that parents will guard their minds as well as their bodies from evil. But I pray now for these children, for _____, and _____, and _____.

My prayer requests:	*God's answers:*

September 15

God's Word to me: Fathers, do not provoke . . . your children . . . or harass them; lest they become discouraged and . . . frustrated . . .

Colossians 3:21 (AMPLIFIED)

Prayer-meditation: This teaching is a bit difficult, Lord, to reconcile with the need to discipline our sometimes stubborn children. However, knowing that the ultimate responsibility for them is Yours enables us to be more relaxed and loving when correction must be given.

My prayer requests:	*God's answers:*

September 16

God's Word to me: I do not pray that Thou shouldst take them out of the world, but that Thou shouldst keep them from the evil one.

John 17:15 (RSV)
(Read also John 17:1–26)

Prayer-meditation: In His high-priestly prayer, Jesus refused to ask the Father for followers secluding themselves from the world, fleeing evil, primarily concerned about their own sanctity or even their Christian growth. Rather we, His people, are to go out into the world to take the initiative against evil, armed with Jesus' own prayer for our protection from Satan.

Let my spirit, Lord, partake of Your boldness as I go out in the strength of the Father's protection.

My prayer requests: | *God's answers:*

September 17

God's Word to me: You are the light of the world ... Nor do men light a lamp and put it under a peck measure but on a lamp stand ...

Matthew 5:14, 15 (AMPLIFIED)

Prayer-meditation: Being a realist, Jesus was impressed only with the waste of lights hidden under peck measures. And His commission to us is not to shut ourselves from the world—rather "to go out *into* all the world". We are to be the salt-preservative in a decaying society, to be light set high on the lamp stand for all to see. For darkness must always flee before the light.

Lord, I would not be a display-light, drawing attention to myself or even to my good works. Praise You, that the Holy Spirit always turns the spotlight on You!

My prayer requests:	*God's answers:*

September 18

God's Word to me: What is man, that Thou art mindful of him? ... For Thou hast made him a little lower than the angels, and hast crowned him with glory, and honour.

Psalm 8:4, 5

Prayer-meditation: Father, You are reminding me this morning that what differentiates men from beasts are Spirit, in-breathed by Creator-Spirit, and human will—the ability to decide and to choose.

Father, thank You for Your insistence that I come to You voluntarily—or not at all. It awes me to realize that not even the Lord of glory will ever forcibly invade that central citadel of my selfhood—where You planted the decision-making process of my will. This mark of Your greatness alone would make me want to worship You.

Thank You for the reality of such freedom in You.

My prayer requests: | *God's answers:*

FREEDOM AND AUTHORITY

September 19

God's Word to me: And they were astonished at His [Jesus'] teaching, for He taught them as one who had authority, and not as the scribes.

Mark 1:22 (RSV)
(Read also Luke 18:18–24)

Prayer-meditation: Lord Jesus, in Your dealings with me I have felt not only the same "authority" mentioned so often in the gospels but also the impact of Your compelling, well-nigh irresistible personality. Yet Your attitude towards me, as towards many another, has always been a sharp hands-off: "It's up to you to decide whether or not you obey. I shall not force you or stampede you. *You* decide." So that was why You could stand silently, watching the rich young ruler walk away from You.

Thank You for demonstrating to us so clearly the difference between true authority and the authoritarianism of force.

My prayer requests:

God's answers:

FREEDOM AND AUTHORITY

September 20

God's Word to me: But I tell you, Do not bind yourself by an oath at all ... And you must not be called masters (leaders), for you have one Master (Leader), the Christ.

Matthew 5:34; 23:10 (AMPLIFIED)

Prayer-meditation: The authority of self-proclaimed prophets, holy men, gurus and leaders of communities demanding vows of obedience is accelerating in our time.

I am grateful, Lord, for Your clear directive here. We are in grave danger whenever we bow our wills and vow to obey any human leader. You *only* are Master and Lord!

My prayer requests:	God's answers:

September 21

God's Word to me: But Peter and the apostles answered, "We must obey God rather than men."

Acts 5:29 (RSV)

Prayer-meditation: Father, thank You for showing me yet other tests to apply to the welter of communities springing up today: Does any leader seek to usurp or subtract from the final supremacy of Jesus' Lordship for me? Would rules of, or vows to this community stand between me and the direct guidance of the Holy Spirit?

I praise You, Father, that You want only sturdy disciples growing steadily in Your strength and Your freedom, dependent upon no man.

My prayer requests:

God's answers:

FALSE PROPHETS

September 22

God's Word to me: Beware of false prophets, which come to you in sheep's clothing, but inwardly they are ravening wolves.

Matthew 7:15
(Read also 1 John 4:1–3)

Prayer-meditation: I especially hear Your warning for our time, Lord, for false prophets are appearing everywhere, often spouting Scripture, offering quick-and-easy promises. Thank You for giving us the definitive test to apply: Anyone who does not confess "that Jesus Christ is come in the flesh is not of God", and we listen to his teaching or follow him with grave danger.

My prayer requests:

God's answers:

September 23

God's Word to me: Let both grow together until the harvest . . . I will say to the reapers, Gather ye together first the tares, and bind them in bundles to burn them . . .

Matthew 13:30

Prayer-meditation: Lord, many of us are troubled about the teaching and witness of some "Christian" groups and communities. Your answer, Lord, is another example of Your ways not being our ways: wheat and tares, truth and error, are growing together in these places. The first young shoots look alike; to pull up the tares ruthlessly would damage the wheat too.

We are to await Your timing, the harvest, when the tares (error, Satan) stand out, easily distinguishable, good only for the fire.

Lord, thank You that You *will* deal with the tares.

My prayer requests:	*God's answers:*

September 24

God's Word to me: Be ye therefore perfect, even as your Father which is in heaven is perfect.

Matthew 5:48

Prayer-meditation:

The expression of Christian character is not good doing, but God-likeness. If the Spirit of God has transformed you within, you will exhibit Divine characteristics in your life, not good human characteristics. God's life in us expresses itself as *God's* life, not as human life trying to be godly . . . and the experience of this works out in the practical details of life . . .

OSWALD CHAMBERS

My prayer requests:

God's answers:

September 25

God's Word to me: Now don't be afraid, go on believing.
Luke 8:50 (PHILLIPS)
(Read also Luke 11:5–13)

Prayer-meditation: When Jesus promised us, "Knock, and it [the door] shall be opened unto you" (Luke 11:9), He implied that there is a time when the door remains shut. So many of us experience this in prayer. We have prayed with all the faith we can muster about a certain problem. But so far there has been no response from God. It is at this point that persistence on our part must go hand in hand with faith. We must keep pressing forward—"go on believing". Jesus never promised us that the door would be opened at our first tap or on our timing.

Lord, strengthen in me this kind of persistence to give me stalwart faith-muscles.

My prayer requests: | *God's answers:*

September 26

God's Word to me: . . . If ye have faith as a grain of mustard seed, ye shall say unto this mountain, Remove hence to yonder place; and it shall remove; and nothing shall be impossible unto you.

Matthew 17:20

Prayer-meditation: Thank You for demonstrating, Lord, that You do not want us to spiritualize our problems and bow down before mountains of evil; that instead You came to demonstrate the art of mountain-moving. We sense in You, Lord, an exuberant faith and a buoyant humour that says, "So that's your problem. There's nothing here that My Father and I can't handle. Come, let us together blast away the mountain."

My prayer requests:

God's answers:

September 27

God's Word to me: . . . So up with your listless hands! Strengthen your weak knees! And make straight paths for your feet to walk in.

Hebrews 12:12, 13 (MOFFATT)

Prayer-meditation: Discouragement and dejection are signs of sickness of spirit (usually not a major illness—just the spiritual sniffles). Sometimes Satan trips us into this sad state by feeding our wounded self-love. Or we have a demanding spirit, conducting ourselves before God like a sulking child demanding what he wants *now*.

Lord, I see it! In my will I choose to give up the luxury of discouragement, and I do now deliberately raise my listless hands to You in praise. Thank you, Lord.

My prayer requests: *God's answers:*

DISCOURAGEMENT

September 28

God's Word to me: Why art thou cast down, O my soul? and why art thou disquieted in me? hope thou in God: for I shall yet praise Him for the help of his countenance.

Psalm 42:5

Prayer-meditation: Some unknown saint has left us this pithy sentence: "All discouragement is from the devil."

One of Satan's prime devices is to trick us into sinning by "giving up" on God.

Lord, with the psalmist, I ask Your light on the *why* of my discouragement. Help me always to remember that despair and negativism are the opposite of hope and faith and a lie from the father of lies.

My prayer requests:

God's answers:

September 29

God's Word to me: And He was there in the wilderness forty days, tempted of Satan; and was with the wild beasts; and the angels ministered unto Him.

Mark 1:13

Prayer-meditation: Thank You, Father, for reminding me that not only does Your Holy Spirit indwell us, but that, as with Jesus, so with us, You have given the angels charge over us to keep us from falling. Thank You for such loving care.

My prayer requests:	*God's answers:*

MY SECRET PLACE OF ABIDING

September 30

God's Word to me: He that dwelleth in the secret place of the most High shall abide under the shadow of the Almighty. I will say of the Lord, He is my refuge and my fortress: my God; in Him will I trust.

Psalm 91:1, 2

Prayer-meditation: These words roll over me like deep water, bringing such refreshment. Even in the midst of a busy office with ringing telephones, sharp voices, tensions and frustrations of people at work, I thank You, Father, that You offer me a "secret place" to enter and abide with You.

My prayer requests: *God's answers:*

SEPTEMBER SUMMARY

October 1

God's Word to me: But the Lord of Hosts, Him you shall regard as holy; let Him be your fear, and let Him be your dread.

Isaiah 8:13 (RSV)
(Read also Genesis 22:12)

Prayer-meditation: The fear of God is a reverence of Him which leads to obedience because of our realization of His power as well as His love for us.

O Lord, I bow before You, honouring You as God. My obedience is given as part of my adoration—in homage to you. It is a small gift in light of who You are.

My prayer requests:	*God's answers:*

October 2

God's Word to me: Because he hath set his love upon Me, therefore will I deliver him: I will set him on high, because he hath known My name.

Psalm 91:14

Prayer-meditation: What a promise, Lord, that it is not because of any of our great works but solely because we set our heart upon You and get to *know* You that You will exalt us. It would seem to be a reward out of all proportion, but then that's the great God You are: "For God so loved the world that He *gave!*" Extravagantly! Beyond human comprehension!

My prayer requests:	*God's answers:*

October 3

God's Word to me: ... Whom do men say that I the Son of man am ... But whom say ye that I am?

Matthew 16:13, 15

Prayer-meditation: Lord, all around me today I hear Your rapier-like question being asked: "Whom do *you* say that I am?" For there is much fascination with other religions, other prophets, gurus, exotic rituals. I am hearing, "What difference will it make to me and my problems to believe that Jesus Christ is the Son of God?" Give me the gift of Your wisdom to communicate Your answer to those around me so that they will hear and heed.

My prayer requests:	*God's answers:*

October 4

God's Word to me: Search me, O God, and know my heart: try me, and know my thoughts: And see if there be any wicked way in me...

Psalm 139:23, 24

Prayer-meditation:

Lord, Thou canst see the hidden things in every heart. If our intentions are good, help us to make them live in good deeds. If what we intend or desire makes us uncomfortable in Thy presence, take it from us and give us the spirit we ought to have that we may do what we ought to do.

PETER MARSHALL

My prayer requests:	*God's answers:*

October 5

God's Word to me: So the Lord alone did lead him, and there was no strange god with him.

Deuteronomy 32:12

Prayer-meditation: Search me, Lord, to show me if I have any other gods that are blocking me from following You: money, clothes, jewellery, home, car, work, the idolatry of any wrong relationship, enslavement to a habit, pride in position—show me, Lord.

My prayer requests:	*God's answers:*

JESUS, THE LIVING WORD

October 6

God's Word to me: You diligently study the Scriptures because you think that by them you possess eternal life. These are the Scriptures that testify about me, yet you refuse to come to me to have life.

John 5:39, 40 (NIV)
(Read also John 1:1, 14)

Prayer-meditation: Lord, You are ever the Realist. You would alert me that being a fine Bible student is good but still not good enough. I have to pass from the written Word to go on to the living Word. This morning I bow at Your feet as the "Word Incarnate".

My prayer requests: | *God's answers:*

October 7

God's Word to me: . . . How beautiful are the feet of them that preach the gospel of peace, and bring glad tidings of good things!
Romans 10:15

Prayer-meditation: Thank You, Lord, for this beautiful commission to service. The apostles continually rejoiced in telling others the good news of salvation through Jesus Christ. Help me to carry this message today with that same joyous Spirit, a clean heart, a straight tongue and a warm smile.

My prayer requests: | *God's answers:*

October 8

God's Word to me: ... I am ready to preach the gospel ... For I am not ashamed of the gospel of Christ: for it is the power of God unto salvation to every one that believeth ...

Romans 1:15, 16

Prayer-meditation: I confess, Lord, that there have been times when I was embarrassed, yes, ashamed to speak Your name. Forgive me for this cowardice; empower me with the courage to testify and the wisdom to know the right moment.

My prayer requests:	*God's answers:*

October 9

God's Word to me: Now therefore go, and I will be with your mouth and teach you what you shall speak.

Exodus 4:12 (RSV)

Prayer-meditation: Lord, this is the reassurance to which I will hold in the days ahead. With You in me I have no fear of people, of places or of the future. Help me to remember this promise and to claim it for particular situations.

My prayer requests:	*God's answers:*

October 10

God's Word to me: ... pray ye therefore the Lord of the harvest, that He would send forth labourers into His harvest.

Luke 10:21
(Read also Luke 10:1–16)

Prayer-meditation: One of the few specific things Jesus ever asked us to pray for was for people who would be His representatives in His ministry of love—labourers to help gather in the harvest. We are to be Jesus' hands, His feet, His voice, the channels of His Spirit for teaching, counselling, ministering, preaching, healing the sick.

Lord, I see that the harvest can never be gathered in unless each of us takes our commission seriously as a personal, daily responsibility. Lead me in this today, Lord.

My prayer requests:	*God's answers:*

October 11

God's Word to me: But if the Spirit of Him that raised up Jesus from the dead dwell in you, He that raised up Christ from the dead shall also quicken your mortal bodies by His Spirit that dwelleth in you.

Romans 8:11

Prayer-meditation: O gracious Spirit, enter into me. Invade every cell of my mortal body, even as Your power invaded the tomb on Resurrection morning to quicken the physical body of Jesus. It is the Spirit that gives life, else the flesh profits nothing. I praise You for this new understanding of Your healing power.

My prayer requests:	*God's answers:*

October 12

God's Word to me: . . . He sent forth His word, and healed them, and delivered them from destruction.

Psalm 107:20 (RSV)
(Read also Matthew 8:16 and Luke 7:1–10)

Prayer-meditation: Lord Jesus, how wonderful that You who created planets and galaxies, and the incredible body of man by sending forth Your Word, also mend and heal our bodies in exactly the same way. Jesus, send forth Your special word of healing and restoration now for _____ and _____, even as You were constantly doing while here in the flesh.

My prayer requests:	God's answers:

October 13

God's Word to me: ... the tongue is a little member, and boasteth great things. Behold, how great a matter a little fire kindleth!

James 3:5

Prayer-meditation: I told myself: this doesn't apply to me, Lord, because I am not given to boasting. But now I realize how often I use my tongue with people for quiet self-promotion. Help me to boast only about You and Your greatness and faithfulness.

My prayer requests:	*God's answers:*

THE TONGUE

God's Word to me: So do not criticize at all . . . rather make up your mind never to put any stumbling block in your brother's way.

1 Corinthians 4:5; Romans 14:13 (MOFFATT)

Prayer-meditation: Lord, since You told us that You came not to condemn us but to save us, who am I to be condemning and critical of others? Lord, cleanse me of the sin of this negative mind-set. Instead, let any concern or discernment of mine flow only into prayers for others.

My prayer requests:	*God's answers:*

October 15

God's Word to me: I tell you, on the day of judgment men will render account for every careless word they utter.

Matthew 12:36 (RSV)

Prayer-meditation: I am beginning to see, Lord, that the gift of speech is precious in Your sight and that You hold me accountable for it. Keep me today from gossip, from thoughtless words that hurt another. Thank you for the gift of speech.

My prayer requests:

God's answers:

THE TONGUE
October 16

God's Word to me: Let your speech always be gracious, seasoned with salt, so that you may know how you ought to answer everyone.

Colossians 4:6 (RSV)

Prayer-meditation: Lord, I've prayed for Your Spirit to enter my heart. Now I ask for You to sweeten the timbre of my voice to reflect perfectly Your love as You use my mouth to comfort the afflicted, to encourage the downhearted, to inspire the defeated.

Let my words to others be only for their upbuilding and encouragement and consolation, savouring of Your neverfailing, loving graciousness to me.

My prayer requests: | *God's answers:*

October 17

God's Word to me: Keep thy heart with all diligence; for out of it are the issues of life. Put away from thee a froward mouth . . .

Proverbs 4:23, 24

Prayer-meditation: I see, Lord, that You hold me responsible for a decision of will to "keep my heart with all diligence". This morning I make that decision even as I ask for Your strength to implement it. Free my mind from any over-emphasis on fleshly desires; keep me free from cynicism, from impure thoughts or fantasies. Help me to bridle my tongue the next time I am tempted to be critical or devious or try to impress another.

My prayer requests: | *God's answers:*

October 18

God's Word to me: Why are you cast down, O my soul, and why are you disquieted within me? Hope in God; for I shall again praise Him, my help and my God.

Psalm 43:5 (RSV)

Prayer-meditation:

Let us not lose the savour of past mercies and past pleasures; but like the voice of a bird singing in the rain, let grateful memory survive in the hour of darkness.

ROBERT LOUIS STEVENSON

My prayer requests:	*God's answers:*

October 19

God's Word to me: Let brotherly love continue. Be not forgetful to entertain strangers: for thereby some have entertained angels unawares.

Hebrews 13:1, 2

Prayer-meditation: With evil so rampant today, Lord, I sometimes tend to avoid contact with strangers. Since I want to be generous and open, give me the gift of discernment so that I will be hospitable to those You send my way.

My prayer requests: | *God's answers:*

THE POWER OF HIS NAME

October 20

God's Word to me: Therefore God has highly exalted Him and bestowed on Him [Jesus] the name which is above every name . . .
Philippians 2:9 (RSV)

Prayer-meditation: Teach me more, Lord, about the incredible power of the name of "Jesus"; how all in heaven bow at this name, and all of hell must drop away when it is spoken. I would scale the heights of adoration in singing or speaking of Jesus. And in every need, every emergency, help me never to forget that the name "Jesus" is my lifeline.

My prayer requests:	*God's answers:*

October 21

God's Word to me: And He hath put a new song in my mouth, even praise unto our God: many shall see it, and fear, and shall trust in the Lord.

Psalm 40:3

Prayer-meditation: It is the wind of Your Spirit, Lord, that brings refreshment and renewal. I ask now for a new song in my mouth, so that I can praise You for all the ways You have blessed my life.

My prayer requests:	God's answers:

October 22

God's Word to me: It is before his own Master that he stands or falls. And he shall stand and be upheld, for the Master—the Lord—is mighty to support him and make him stand.

Romans 14:4 (AMPLIFIED)

Prayer-meditation: Lord, I need this strong word of encouragement this morning. You know how troubled I have been about _____. It is hard to stand by and watch one I care about so deeply going down such a destructive path.

I praise You that Your undergirding of _____'s life cannot and will not fail.

My prayer requests:	*God's answers:*

October 23

God's Word to me: [And Moses said] . . . "Fear not, stand firm, and see the salvation of the Lord, which He will work for you today . . ."

Exodus 14:13 (RSV)

Prayer-meditation: O Spirit of God, I look to You to do in me what I cannot do for myself. As this day presents new demands, I will live in You, and You will do through me what is required. I must not try, but trust; must not struggle, but rest. Then will Your salvation be seen.

My prayer requests:	God's answers:

October 24

God's Word to me: . . . thy life will I give unto thee for a prey in all places whither thou goest.

Jeremiah 45:5

Prayer-meditation: Father, enable me to abandon my life to You as Jesus abandoned His life to You when He suffered the cross. For only then can I see this beautiful Scripture become real. As Your life, flowing through the Holy Spirit, becomes my life, I will truly become a prey, attracting to me all the good of Your perfect will—whatever you want me to experience at any time, in any place.

My prayer requests:	*God's answers:*

October 25

God's Word to me: Be glad, O sons of Zion, and rejoice in the Lord, your God ...

Joel 2:23 (RSV)

Prayer-meditation: We praise and thank You, our God, for the prosperity received at Your hand. Your kindness has brought us all we need: loving friends and family, health, and successes in our undertakings. Your mercy and grace have been on our lives. You are a good and great God. Praise Your holy name!

My prayer requests:	*God's answers:*

October 26

God's Word to me: ... not having a righteousness of my own ...
Philippians 3:9 (RSV)

Prayer-meditation:
> Nothing in my hands I bring,
> Simply to Thy cross I cling.
>   AUGUSTUS M. TOPLADY, 1775

Lord Jesus, I see that the stain of sin inherited from our ancestor Adam is not so much immorality and dishonesty as it is claiming my right to myself, to do what I please, to be my own god (Genesis 3:5). It was to put *that* away that You died on the Cross for me.

Therefore, I have no "rights" because to You alone I owe life itself, every breath I draw, the ability to think, to move, to love, every talent I possess.

Your grace and goodness to all of us is incredible! Lord, I bow before You in adoration.

My prayer requests:	*God's answers:*

October 27

God's Word to me: For the grace of God—His unmerited favour and blessing—has . . . [appeared] for the deliverance from sin and the eternal salvation for all mankind.

Titus 2:11 (AMPLIFIED)

Prayer-meditation: Lord, I have had to learn the hard way that I am in the gravest danger from Satan whenever I allow myself to think things like, "I deserve to spend some money on myself", or "I deserve to make this 'Be-Good-to-Me Day'." Does this open the door to Satan because I am reverting to the primary sin of the human race—my "right" to myself, and thus denying Your sacrifice on the cross?

Thank You for the truth: that I deserve nothing from Your hands, and that every good gift comes to me by pure grace.

Lord, keep me from ever falling into Satan's "deserving" trap again.

My prayer requests: | *God's answers:*

October 28

God's Word to me: . . . and lo, I am with you all the days—perpetually, uniformly and on every occasion . . .

Matthew 28:20 (AMPLIFIED)

Prayer-meditation: You, Lord, are more than an idea or an influence, more than a guiding power: You are an alive, real Person—my Companion and Friend. And there is a constancy about your presence which does not depend on my feelings or on what I am doing. Thank You for Your faithfulness to me.

My prayer requests:	*God's answers:*

October 29

God's Word to me: But Peter and the apostles [when accused by the High Priest] answered, "We must obey God rather than men."
Acts 5:29 (RSV)

Prayer-meditation: Imagine the fearless confidence of these apostles given them by the Holy Spirit as they stood before the council in Jerusalem and took their stand for Jesus Christ!

When the moment of testing comes for me, Lord, I too want the infusion of the Spirit's power for this kind of obedience.

My prayer requests:	*God's answers:*

GOD, OUR REFUGE

October 30

God's Word to me: God is our refuge and strength, a very present help in trouble.

Psalm 46:1

Prayer-meditation: Lord, what comfort this verse has brought to me. Not only are You my "hiding place" in times of trouble, but You are even my "fount of joy" in the great moments of fulfilment. I rejoice to know that You are also my Father, Creator, Redeemer and ever-present Lord of my life.

My prayer requests:	God's answers:

October 31

God's Word to me: . . . Holy Father, keep through Thine own name those whom Thou hast given Me, that they may be one, as we are.

John 17:11

Prayer-meditation: "Holy Father." Jesus reaches to the ultimate of Your Sovereignty to plead our cause. He knew that Satan attacks those who belong to You, not the worldlings. We, Your own people, need Jesus' intercession for our strengthening, protection, and steady growth as we are planted in You.

Thank You for the reassurance that as we are kept in the holiness of God, we will be transformed into Your likeness—"that they may be one, as we are".

My prayer requests:

God's answers:

OCTOBER SUMMARY

November 1

God's Word to me: . . . be not afraid, neither be thou dismayed: for the Lord thy God is with thee whithersoever thou goest.

Joshua 1:9

Prayer-meditation: The world is a jungle today, Lord. But when I enter it, I go forth in confidence, knowing that You are with me and that Your protecting angels surround me.

My prayer requests: *God's answers:*

TRIBULATION
November 2

God's Word to me: . . . In the world ye shall have tribulation: but be of good cheer; I have overcome the world.

John 16:33
(Read also John 17:15)

Prayer-meditation: Thank You, Lord, for Your realism. You have never promised to take us Christians out of the world or to be an insurance policy against all trouble. We praise You for this sure promise of a strengthening and overcoming victory in tribulation. No wonder we are to be of good cheer!

My prayer requests: *God's answers:*

November 3

God's Word to me: He who loves money will not be satisfied with money; nor he who loves wealth, with gain: this also is vanity.
Ecclesiastes 5:10 (RSV)

Prayer-meditation: Father, You are helping me to see the pattern of evil that results from love of money, from greed, vanity, selfishness, lust, corruption. I see this about myself, but I am also deeply troubled about what I see in our nation. A "me-first" or "my in-group-first" philosophy of unabashed selfishness and greed is masquerading under lofty, pretentious jargon about self-fulfilment.

Father, save us from the wreckage that such selfishness brings. Show us before it is too late that we, as a people, rise or fall, prosper or go down to destruction together.

My prayer requests:

God's answers:

ELECTION DAY

November 4

God's Word to me: For to us a child is born, to us a Son is given; and the government will be upon His shoulder . . .

Isaiah 9:6 (RSV)

Prayer-meditation:

Lord Jesus, we ask You to guide the people of this nation as they exercise their dearly bought privilege of franchise. May it neither be ignored unthinkingly nor undertaken lightly. As citizens all over this land go to the ballot boxes . . . we ask Thee to lead this country in the paths where You would have her walk.

PETER MARSHALL

My prayer requests:	*God's answers:*

November 5

God's Word to me: Of the increase of His government . . . there will be no end . . . to establish it, and to uphold it with justice and with righteousness from this time forth and for evermore.

Isaiah 9:7 (RSV)

Prayer-meditation:

Father-God, help those who have been elected to public office to understand the real source of their mandate —a mandate given by no party machine, received at no polling booth, but given by God; a mandate to govern wisely and well; a mandate to represent God at the heart of the nation; a mandate to do good in the Name of Him under whom this nation was established.

PETER MARSHALL

My prayer requests:	*God's answers:*

PERSEVERANCE

November 6

God's Word to me: And ye shall seek me, and find me, when ye shall search for me with all your heart.

Jeremiah 29:13
(Read also Luke 11:9, 10)

Prayer-meditation: I have seen in you, O Father, incredible perseverance in seeking for me, as you have looked for me and found me no matter where I have sought to hide. I know you would undertake painstaking diligence to find me again. Grant that I, in return, might have that same kind of fervour in seeking for You. I want the totality of my being involved. Quicken my heart and stir my mind to become a true seeker after You.

My prayer requests:	*God's answers:*

November 7

God's Word to me: ... slowly, steadily, surely, the time approaches when the vision will be fulfilled. If it seems slow, do not despair, for these things will surely come to pass. Just be patient! They will not be overdue a single day!

Habakkuk 2:3 (TLB)

Prayer-meditation: How often, Lord, I have asked You to give me a vision of Your purpose and plan for my life. But true to my instant and active generation, I am impatient with Your majestic timing. Thank You for reminding me that in Your sovereign knowledge and power, You are never even a minute late. Give me the patience not to run ahead of You but to wait for You to fulfil in my life Your dream for me.

My prayer requests:

God's answers:

DENYING MYSELF

November 8

God's Word to me: Then said Jesus unto His disciples, If any man will come after Me, let him deny himself, and take up his cross, and follow Me.

Matthew 16:24

Prayer-meditation: Self-denial will occur as we walk in obedience, giving ourselves away to God and to man in need.

Jesus, we can learn from You how to carry our crosses. You bore Yours out of love for the Father and because You knew the glory it would accomplish. Grant us that same vision.

My prayer requests: | *God's answers:*

November 9

God's Word to me: And whosoever of you will be the chiefest, shall be servant of all.

Mark 10:44
(Read also Mark 10:32–45)

Prayer-meditation: Until now, Jesus, I never knew I had a "power complex". To be a servant, to be submissive to another, to keep a servant's heart, goes against my grain, Lord. I need Your grace to make it possible.

My prayer requests:	God's answers:

November 10

God's Word to me: Ye cannot drink the cup of the Lord, and the cup of devils: ye cannot be partakers of the Lord's table, and the table of devils.

1 Corinthians 10:21
(Read also Matthew 6:24; Genesis 41:14–24)

Prayer-meditation: Jesus, You said we could not serve God and mammon. My life so far is proof of that. Deliver me, Lord, from my lust for tangible security that You may have freedom in me to work Your work of eternal security.

My prayer requests:	God's answers:

November 11

God's Word to me: ... He [the Lord] has sent Me to bind up the brokenhearted ...

Isaiah 61:1 (RSV)
(Read also Matthew 5:4 and Revelation 21:4)

Prayer-meditation: You have suffered grief as we have, Lord, and have Yourself been broken. It eases our pain to have You share our plight—enter into it with us. You know how to comfort us with the right words, the right counsel to give us as You wrap our hearts with Your love.

I praise You that though our "weeping may endure for a night ... joy cometh in the morning" (Psalm 30:5).

My prayer requests: | *God's answers:*

THE DISCIPLINE OF PRUNING

November 12

God's Word to me: Every branch in Me that beareth not fruit He taketh away: and every branch that beareth fruit, He purgeth it, that it may bring forth more fruit.

John 15:2

Prayer-meditation: The two trees were only a few feet apart, but they were separated by a fence because they had different owners. One tree was very straight, its branches heavy laden with beautiful, big, red apples. The other tree was scraggy, unkept, too weary to feed and hold its fruit. A pitiful few infested apples lay on the ground around it.

Lord, when the "pruning" hurts and I cry out, don't cease Your pruning, for I too, desire to bear Your fruit.

My prayer requests:	*God's answers:*

November 13

God's Word to me: Beloved, I beseech you as aliens and exiles to abstain from the passions of the flesh that wage war against your soul.

1 Peter 2:11 (RSV)

Prayer-meditation: Lord, You call us to an unalterable ethical standard. It sets us apart as alien residents in an oft-times hostile and ridiculing world. But we renounce all the false and evil attitudes of a life outside of Christ, and choose to be ambassadors of His kingdom here on earth, no matter the cost.

My prayer requests:	*God's answers:*

TAKE MY WILL, LORD

November 14

God's Word to me: . . . giving all diligence, add to your faith virtue . . .

2 Peter 1:5

Prayer-meditation: Jesus has given us salvation and the Holy Spirit indwells us. But a life of victory and power hinges on three things: an act, a purpose, and a habit.

Lord, by Your Holy Spirit maintain in me a continuing act of surrender to Your Lordship. Help me to keep a steady purpose in everything, willing to do as You would wish. Enable me to build a daily habit of being alone with You, my Bible open, my knees bent, and my spirit united with Yours.

My prayer requests:

God's answers:

November 15

God's Word to me: Strengthened with all might, according to His glorious power, unto all patience and longsuffering with joyfulness.

Colossians 1:11

Prayer-meditation: From the lives of the apostles we learn that endurance was one of the chief credentials of God's "sent ones". To remain steadfast under continuous pressure was a test of their calling.

The situation has not changed. We who follow Jesus today find, as did the apostles, that spiritual power, along with joy and patience, is manifest as we faithfully endure.

Lord, be my strength to endure joyously.

My prayer requests:	*God's answers:*

ENDURANCE

November 16

God's Word to me: Fear not ... for I am with you; do not look around you in terror and be dismayed, for I am your God. I will strengthen and harden you [to difficulties] ... For I, the Lord your God, hold your right hand ...

Isaiah 41:10, 13 (AMPLIFIED)

Prayer-meditation: I begin to understand that Your way is not to remove my difficulties immediately but to give me adequacy to cope through the strengthening of Your Spirit. That is why You would take from me self-pity, all "what-ifs", any wallowing in remorse, any thought of "what I deserve". Praise You, Father, for Your strong right hand holding me up.

My prayer requests:	*God's answers:*

November 17

God's Word to me: . . . the god of this world hath blinded the minds of them which believe not, lest the light of the glorious gospel of Christ, who is the image of God, should shine unto them.

2 Corinthians 4:4

Prayer-meditation: Jesus, You said that we were to let our light shine for "the darkness could not overcome the Light". Make me willing, Lord, to have You so fill my life with Your Light that the darkness of disbelief will be thrust from the minds of those I meet.

My prayer requests:	God's answers:

GIVING UP CONTROL

November 18

God's Word to me: And the serpent said unto the woman, Ye shall not surely die: For God doth know that in the day ye eat thereof, then your eyes shall be opened, and ye shall be às gods, knowing good and evil.

Genesis 3:4, 5

Prayer-meditation: O Lord, this has been the bane of my life—wanting to be a "god", to have power over people. Your Word shows me it is the Tempter working on me as he did on Eve. Deliver me from my adversary, Lord, that I may walk in love and peace with my fellow-man and not try to control them.

My prayer requests:	God's answers:

November 19

God's Word to me: And the glory of the Lord abode upon mount Sinai . . . And the sight of the glory of the Lord was like devouring fire on the top of the mount . . .

Exodus 24:16, 17
(Read also Exodus 24:1–18)

Prayer-meditation: Lord God Almighty, there are times when chatty familiarity with You or swinging, hand-clapping choruses are out of place. At such moments we can only bow before You in awe-struck reverence, able to say only "My Lord and my God!"

My prayer requests:	*God's answers:*

O THOU WHO CHANGEST NOT

November 20

God's Word to me: While the earth remaineth, seedtime and harvest, and cold and heat, and summer and winter, and day and night shall not cease.

Genesis 8:22

Prayer-meditation: The revolving seasons, the inevitability of day and night, eloquently speak to me, Father, of our God who changest not . . .

> God of our life, through all the circling years, We trust in Thee.
> In all the past, through all our hopes and fears, Thy hand we see.
> With each new day, when morning lifts the veil,
> We own thy mercies, Lord, which never fail.

HUGH T. KERR

My prayer requests:

God's answers:

November 21

God's Word to me: . . . and be ye kind one to another, tender-hearted, forgiving one another, even as God for Christ's sake hath forgiven you.

Ephesians 4:32

Prayer-meditation: Lord, I confess that my heart is not always tender and kind towards those who do not love me or please me. Since a melting process is needed inside my heart, give me as a gift, Your tenderness, Your kindness, Your generosity of Spirit.

My prayer requests:	*God's answers:*

November 22

God's Word to me: And as you wish that men would do to you, do so to them . . . and you will be sons of the Most High; for He is kind to the ungrateful and the selfish. Be merciful, even as your Father is merciful.

Luke 6:31, 35, 36 (RSV)
(Read also Matthew 18:23–35)

Prayer-meditation:

    Give us grace and strength to forebear and to persevere. Offenders, give us grace to accept and to forgive offenders. Forgetful ourselves, help us to bear cheerfully the forgetfulness of others . . . Purge out of every heart the lurking grudge.

ROBERT LOUIS STEVENSION

My prayer requests:	God's answers:

November 23

God's Word to me: . . . [Love] does not rejoice at wrong, but rejoices in the right.

1 Corinthians 13:6 (RSV)

Prayer-meditation: Lord, I confess that even with members of my family whom I love, I sometimes would rather see them fail than succeed. Help me to see this for what it is—the sin of jealousy—and hand it over to You for forgiveness and cleansing.

My prayer requests:	*God's answers:*

November 24

God's Word to me: . . . all Mine are thine, and thine are Mine . . . Give, and it shall be given unto you; good measure, pressed down, and shaken together, and running over, shall men give into your bosom. For with the same measure that ye mete withal it shall be measured to you again.

John 17:10; Luke 6:38

Prayer-meditation: I praise you, Father, for creating a world not only supplied with everything we need, but also aflame with beauty lavished everywhere. Enable me to grasp deep in my spirit that there is never lack in You, Lord, only love of beauty and opulent abundance; and that we set this abundance in motion only by giving.

I praise You that as I give, supply—"pressed down and running over"—will be returned to me as surely as the tide must return to the shore.

My prayer requests:	*God's answers:*

November 25

God's Word to me: And that which fell among thorns are they, which, when they have heard, go forth, and are choked with cares and riches and pleasures of this life, and bring no fruit to perfection.

Luke 8:14

Prayer-meditation: Thank You, Lord, for showing me that affluence can be a Satan-led trip to a sterile life. You have given me enough abundance to understand that the care of too many possessions can choke me by complicating it. Show me how to simplify my life on the basis of Your priorities, so that I too can bring forth fruit.

My prayer requests:

God's answers:

November 26

God's Word to me: When they were filled, He said unto His disciples, Gather up the fragments that remain, that nothing be lost.

John 6:12

Prayer-meditation: Lord Jesus, this teaching says to me that even though our Father "owns all the cattle on a thousand hills", nothing is to be wasted. It must sicken You, Lord, to see the extravagant waste of food by a small portion of the world's population while the larger percentage are hungry and undernourished. Lord, help me to appreciate Your supply for my needs, and to use properly as a careful steward the abundance You supply.

My prayer requests:	*God's answers:*

November 27

God's Word to me: When you reap the harvest of your land, you shall not reap your field to its very border, neither shall you gather the gleanings after your harvest . . . it shall be for the sojourner, the fatherless, and the widow.

Leviticus 19:9; Deuteronomy 24:20 (RSV)
(Read also Deuteronomy 24:19–22)

Prayer-meditation: Father, from the days of the Pilgrims even unto now, You have dealt bountifully with us in this good land. Help us never to take this rain of mercies for granted, nor attribute them solely to *our* efforts.

So may we carry our gratitude into the grace of sharing. What lonely or needy ones would You have sit at our table? Lead us to them, Father.

My prayer requests:

God's answers:

THE CONDITIONS OF HIS PROVISION

November 28

God's Word to me: And all the tithe of the land, whether of the seed of the land, or of the fruit of the tree, is the Lord's: it is holy unto the Lord.

Leviticus 27:30

Prayer-meditation: Your word here is clear: ten per cent of my total income belongs to You anyway. When I hang on to it, I am robbing You. This is a holy obligation, Lord. From now on help me to fulfil this prime condition of Your provision.

My prayer requests:	*God's answers:*

November 29

God's Word to me: And David danced before the Lord with all his might . . . let all the people praise Thee . . .

> *2 Samuel 6:14; Psalms 67:3*
> *(Read also 2 Samuel 6:12–23)*

Prayer-meditation: Lord, I see that Your servant David, a master of praise, had immense variety in worship because he allowed the Spirit of God to direct it. Sometimes there was overflowing, uninhibited joy; at times, quietness—silence; at other times, reverence clothed in the towering words of the liturgy of the "Church Militant and Triumphant".

Lord, give us too, the flexibility of Your Spirit in worship.

My prayer requests:	God's answers:

THE STRONG MEAT OF THE GOSPEL

November 30

God's Word to me: But strong meat belongeth to them that are of full age . . . who . . . have their senses exercised to discern both good and evil.

Hebrews 5:14

Prayer-meditation: Lord, I seek the strong meat and deeper truths of Your teaching. Stretch my mind to receive more knowledge, increase my understanding of Your word about right and wrong and cleanse my body so that it can be a temple for Your Spirit.

My prayer requests:	*God's answers:*

NOVEMBER SUMMARY

December 1

God's Word to me: For God so loved the world, that He gave His only begotten Son, that whosoever believeth in Him should not perish, but have everlasting life.

John 3:16
(Read also John 3:1–21)

Prayer-meditation: Lord, I believe that You are the Christ, the Son of the living God. But I know that "the belief" You were speaking about to Nicodemus was not mere intellectual acceptance of the fact of Your divinity (followed by formally joining some church) but rather making You absolute Master of my life. At any point where I am still not ready to bow the will, Lord, make me at least willing to be willing. I ask You to do that work in me.

My prayer requests:	God's answers:

December 2

God's Word to me: As the Lord hath been with my lord the king...

1 Kings 1:37
(Read also 1 Samuel 26)

Prayer-meditation: David was every inch a king: as a shepherd lad putting a lion or bear to flight; bringing down the giant Goliath in the name of the Lord of hosts; leading the mighty warriors of Saul. But when, as a fugitive from Saul, he suddenly found his pursuer at his mercy, David refused to strike the killing blow. This was true kingship, for he who cannot control his own spirit is no king.

The Lord Jesus voluntarily laid down His life that He might take it up again. My Lord and my King!

My prayer requests:	*God's answers:*

THE PRIORITY OF THE KINGDOM

December 3

God's Word to me: Seek ye first the kingdom of God, and His righteousness; and all these things shall be added unto you.

Matthew 6:33

Prayer-meditation: Lord, I pray for the faith to believe that if I get my priorities straight by putting Your kingdom first, You will provide for all my lesser needs.

My prayer requests:	*God's answers:*

THE PRIORITY OF THE KINGDOM

December 4

God's Word to me: Moreover, because I have set my affection on the house of my God, in addition to all I have prepared for the holy house, I have a private treasure of gold and silver which I give for the house of my God.

1 Chronicles 29:3 (AMPLIFIED)
(*Read also Luke 21:2–4*)

Prayer-meditation: As I look at Your righteousness, Jesus, it seems to demand of me a total commitment of all things internal and external. You know there are possessions and securities to which I cling. I give You permission to take my will and change it so that I *want* to commit all things and all of myself to You.

My prayer requests:	God's answers:

December 5

God's Word to me: But when the husbandmen saw him, they reasoned among themselves, saying, This is the heir: come, let us kill him, that the inheritance may be ours.

Luke 20:14

Prayer-meditation: Lord, we seek Your guidance. You give it and also multiply Your gifts to us. Then we allow greed to overcome gratitude and cut You off from Your portion. I'm as guilty as those husbandmen, Lord. I hand my greed over to You. Transform it into love for You.

My prayer requests: | *God's answers:*

PROTECTION

December 6

God's Word to me: Put on the whole armour of God, that you may be able to stand against the wiles of the devil.

Ephesians 6:11 (RSV)

Prayer-meditation: The protection devices of the world are not enough to guarantee our safety, Lord. Teach me how Your armour protects me against the virulent forces of evil, so that in the attack I will be able to hold my ground firmly and securely.

My prayer requests:	*God's answers:*

December 7

God's Word to me: ... He who has seen Me has seen the Father ...
John 14:9 (RSV)
(Read also John 14:1–14)

Prayer-meditation: God, pure Spirit, had a problem: how could He bridge the chasm between the Creator and the created? How could He show man what He is really like? God solved this problem in the incarnation. Jesus broke into history; He became one of us. If we want to know what the Father is like, we have but to look at Jesus.

Father, I thank You that the crystal stream of Jesus' life so clearly and perfectly mirrors You. I thank You for understanding my human limitations and making gracious provision for my every need.

My prayer requests:	*God's answers:*

TEMPTATION
December 8

God's Word to me: . . . He [Jesus] said unto them, Pray that ye enter not into temptation.

Luke 22:40

Prayer-meditation: As Christians our desire is that God will be glorified by the fulfilment of His purpose in our lives. So our Father clearly defines for us the functional boundaries of our relationship with Him—just as He did with Adam and Eve. As we accept His loving directive, God and man live in harmony. But then Satan drops a subtle, contrary point of view into our minds: "Ye shall not surely die, but ye shall be as gods . . ." capable of even closer fellowship! Denounce it quickly and decisively; tell Satan to take that temptation to Jesus!

Lord, be my Watchguard and my Deliverer from all rationalization.

My prayer requests:

God's answers:

December 9

God's Word to me: . . . and it was winter.

John 10:22

Prayer-meditation: This morning the earth is covered with a fluffy white blanket; icicles hang from the eaves of the house. Even the fire hydrant wears a cocky white cap. I saw a cardinal, brilliant and red against the dazzling white.

Thank You, Father, for such beauty outside with the cosiness of home within; for fire on the hearth, the singing kettle on the hob; for firelight and candlelight along with modern conveniences; for family around me—and friends.

And bless all those this day who are cold and cheerless, and who sorely need help and encouragement.

My prayer requests:	*God's answers:*

December 10

God's Word to me: Beloved, if God so loved us, we ought also to love one another.

1 John 4:11

Prayer-meditation:

> All praise to our redeeming Lord, Who joins us by His
>   grace,
> And bids us, each to each restored, Together seek His
>   face.
> He bids us build each other up; And, gathered into one,
> To our high calling's glorious hope, We hand in hand
>   go on.

CHARLES WESLEY, 1788

Lord, thank You for the reminder that there is opportunity given here for us to experience a foretaste of heaven as we work through difficult relationships and enter into Your reconciliation.

My prayer requests:	*God's answers:*

December 11

God's Word to me: ... let us love one another: for love is of God; and every one that loveth is born of God, and knoweth God.

1 John 4:7

Prayer-meditation: O Lord, for those precious and rich friendships which are rooted and grounded in You, I give You thanks. The richness of Your love discovered through these relationships helps make life full and meaningful. Continue to be the binding force and origin of our love. But teach us how to avoid selfishness and possessiveness, for we must be free to be Your love for others as well.

My prayer requests:	God's answers:

TEMPTATION

December 12

God's Word to me: There hath no temptation taken you but such as is common to man: but God is faithful, Who will not suffer you to be tempted above that ye are able; but will with the temptation also make a way to escape, that ye may be able to bear it.

1 Corinthians 10:13

Prayer-meditation: Thank You, Lord, for this great promise: that You know me all through, even my limitations; that even this promise leaves me without the usual excuse, "I couldn't help it," and without the luxury of any self-pity.

Today make me alert to temptation, to Your strengthening to bear it, and to Your appointed way of escape.

My prayer requests:	*God's answers:*

December 13

God's Word to me: Set your affection on things above, not on things on the earth.

Colossians 3:2

Prayer-meditation: Paul is not telling us to live in a state of super-spirituality, for that would be hyprocrisy. Jesus loved the world of nature: working with His hands in the Nazareth carpentry shop; playing with children; and all the ordinary things that we enjoy. But His highest affection was to His Father, and that is where ours is to be.

Lord, set the desire of my heart too, on Your Kingdom and Your righteousness.

My prayer requests: *God's answers:*

December 14

God's Word to me: Be ye kind one to another, tenderhearted ...
Ephesians 4:32

Prayer-meditation: Lord, when another person gets in my way or bothers me today, remind me to respond to him or her with Your tenderness and compassion.

My prayer requests:	*God's answers:*

December 15

God's Word to me: O God, Thou art my God, I yearn for Thee, body and soul, I thirst, I long for Thee, like a land without water, weary, dry.

Psalm 63:1 (MOFFATT)

Prayer-meditation:

'Tis not to ask for gifts alone, I kneel in prayer before
   His Throne;
But, seeking fellowship divine, I feel His love, and know
   it mine, When I can pray.

I ought to pray, because my voice, Can make the
   Father's heart rejoice;
He loves His child, and He will meet, And hold
   communication sweet, With one who prays.

MARY RUSSELL OLIVANT, 1852

My prayer requests: | *God's answers:*

December 16

God's Word to me: But we trusted ... and beside all this, today is the third day ... Simon Peter saith unto them, I go a fishing ...
Luke 24:21; John 21:3

Prayer-meditation: The apostles had been with their Master for three years: hearing His teaching, witnessing incredible miracles, feeling the impact of His personality. Yet now they were dejected men ... "We had hoped ... He promised to rise on the third day." In despair Peter grumbled, "It's no use. I'm going back to my old life—fishing."

Yet there was the risen Lord, walking beside the disciples on the road to Emmaus; standing on the beach waiting for Peter.

Open my eyes, Lord, to see You beside me too—now.

My prayer requests: | *God's answers:*

December 17

God's Word to me: Again, ye have heard that it hath been said by them of old time, Thou shalt not forswear thyself, but shalt perform unto the Lord thine oaths.

Matthew 5:33

Prayer-meditation: Lord Jesus, forgive me for the many times I have made promises to people to pray for them and have then forgotten to do so. Help me to remember that to make a promise is to give an oath as unto You, and that the obligation to fulfil it is clear and binding.

My prayer requests: *God's answers:*

RECEIVE HIS FORGIVENESS

December 18

God's Word to me: ... Neither do I condemn thee: go, and sin no more.

John 8:11

Prayer-meditation: Jesus never berates or belittles us. He describes as sin any deed or memory that hampers or binds human personality—as our "missing the mark" of His wonderful plan for our life and thus wasting our great potential. The problem is that all our past sins, if unforgiven, are still in the present tense because they still are a part of us.

Lord, I thank You for the immediacy of Your forgiveness, the completeness of Your cleansing, the gladness of Your restoration, and for You, Lord Jesus, who made this possible.

My prayer requests:	*God's answers:*

December 19

God's Word to me: . . . and him who comes to Me I will most certainly not cast out—I will never, no never reject one of them who comes to Me.

John 6:37 (AMPLIFIED)

Prayer-meditation: Lord, what a glorious word to remember always for myself and for others. What joy to know that there is no human life so sordid, no sin so terrible, no case so extreme that the blood of Your cross does not cover it, that Your love does not embrace it. O Saviour, thank You for coming to earth to rescue us from ourselves.

My prayer requests:	*God's answers:*

December 20

God's Word to me: I have blotted out, as a thick cloud, thy transgressions, and, as a cloud, thy sins: return unto Me; for I have redeemed thee.

Isaiah 44:22

Prayer-meditation: I praise You for being a forgiving Lord. But I see that there is one condition: returning unto You. I do return, Lord, and kneel again at Your feet. Take my life, make it and mould it as You will. And now I claim this great promise. Thank You for unburdening me of so great a weight.

My prayer requests:

God's answers:

AND FORGIVE ONE ANOTHER

December 21

God's Word to me: And forgive us our debts, as we forgive our debtors.

Matthew 6:12
(Read also Matthew 5:21–26)

Prayer-meditation: It is a startling truth, Father, that You can forgive me my sins (which are so numerous) only to the extent that I am willing to forgive my fellow human beings.

But how great it is that the minute I, a prodigal, turn back to You in repentance, You come running down the road to meet me. And also, Father, I am learning that whenever I am willing for Christ's sake to go more than halfway to mend a quarrel, You rush joyously ahead of me to prepare the way. Thank You that it matters so much to You!

My prayer requests:

God's answers:

AND FORGIVE ONE ANOTHER

December 22

God's Word to me: . . . forbearing one another and, if one has a complaint against another, forgiving each other; as the Lord has forgiven you, so you also must forgive.

Colossians 3:13 (RSV)
(Read also Matthew 18:21–35)

Prayer-meditation: Lord, as I consider forgiving _____, there's a wrenching that goes on because it will cost me my sense of justice. My anger and resentment seem a proper retaliation for the wrong done me. And yet, your command is there: to forgive. Therefore, in my will I *do* forgive, in spite of all my emotions shrieking to the contrary. I will hold on to this grudge no longer and ask You to help me wipe the slate clean.

My prayer requests:	*God's answers:*

December 23

God's Word to me: We know that we have passed out of death into life, because we love the brethren.

1 John 3:14
(Read also 1 John 3:11–18)

Prayer-meditation: Father, You have commanded that I forgive. I have honestly tried, but my resentments against _____ keep coming back. Here in my open hands I hold my wrong feelings and emotions. I can control my will but not my emotions. It is my will to have You take from me hurt feelings and unforgiveness. Through a miracle of Your grace, sweeten my heart and richly bless this one whom I have disliked.

My prayer requests:	*God's answers:*

December 24

God's Word to me: And she [Mary] gave birth to her first-born Son and wrapped Him in swaddling clothes, and laid Him in a manger, because there was no place for them in the inn.

Luke 2:7 (RSV)

Prayer-meditation:

O come to my heart, Lord Jesus;
There is room in my heart for Thee.

EMILY E. S. ELLIOTT

Lord Jesus, I would find room in the inn of my heart for You this Christmastide. Even as we invite You, our Saviour, to be born again in us, so go with us to be our Companion in all that we do. And in the days ahead, let us be Your bridge and Your ambassadors to others.

My prayer requests:

God's answers:

December 25

God's Word to me: For unto you is born this day in the city of David a Saviour, which is Christ the Lord. And this shall be a sign unto you: Ye shall find the babe wrapped in swaddling clothes, lying in a manger.

Luke 2:11, 12

Prayer-meditation: Dear Lord, since Christ was born in a simple Bethlehem manger, I will celebrate today by acts of simplicity; a prayer of praise, partaking of the sacraments, a demonstration of love as I give gifts to others from my heart.

My prayer requests:	*God's answers:*

December 26

God's Word to me: And the shepherds returned, glorifying and praising God for all the things that they had heard and seen, as it was told unto them.

Luke 2:20

Prayer-meditation:

O Lord Jesus, we thank You for the joys of this season, for the divine love that was shed abroad among men when You first came as a little child. Help each one of us to keep Christmas alive in our hearts and in our homes, that it may continue to glow, to shed its warmth, to speak its message during all the bleak days of winter. So may Christmas linger with us, even as You, Lord, are beside us the whole year through.

PETER MARSHALL

My prayer requests:	God's answers:

December 27

God's Word to me: Bless . . . the Lord, O my soul, and forget not [one of] all His benefits.

Who forgives [every one of] all your iniquities, Who heals [each of] all your diseases;

Who redeems your life from the pit and corruption; Who beautifies, dignifies, and crowns you with loving kindness and tender mercies.

Psalm 103:2–4 (AMPLIFIED)

Prayer-meditation: Lord, with such joyous reassurance as this, Your own Word to me, my praise rises like a fountain. As I let my mind roam back over this year, I find it studded with Your mercies, blessed by many an answer to prayer, crowned indeed with Your loving kindness. Thank You, thank You!

My prayer requests:	*God's answers:*

THE GIFT OF FAITH

December 28

God's Word to me: For by the grace . . . given to me I warn every one among you not to estimate and think of himself more highly than he ought . . . but to rate his ability . . . each according to the degree of faith apportioned by God to him.

Romans 12:3 (AMPLIFIED)

Prayer-meditation: This morning Your Word tells me that my rating in the Kingdom of God is not on the basis of my good works but on the degree of my faith (to what extent I believe and trust You to handle my life and the lives of those I love). I am learning also that in Your eyes, Lord, unbelief is the greatest sin of all.

Therefore, very simply, Lord, I ask You for the gift of faith—the capacity, the ability, and the stamina—to trust You for anything the New Year holds. Thank You that this greatest gift of faith is Yours to bestow.

My prayer requests:	*God's answers:*

December 29

God's Word to me: Wherefore seeing we also are compassed about with so great a cloud of witnesses . . .

Hebrews 12:1

Prayer-meditation:

Let saints on earth unite to sing, With those to glory gone; For all the servants of our King, In earth and heaven are one:

E'en now by faith we join our hands, With those that went before, And greet the blood-redeemed bands, On the eternal shore.

CHARLES WESLEY, 1788

What tremendous encouragement, Lord Jesus, to know that so many of Your followers have kept the faith and have become witnesses at home with You in the eternal household of faith. I look forward to joining You there.

My prayer requests:	*God's answers:*

FAITH FOR THE LONG VIEW

December 30

God's Word to me: All flesh shall see the salvation of God.

Luke 3:6

Prayer-meditation:

God of our Fathers and our God, give us the faith to believe in the ultimate triumph of righteousness . . . We pray for the bifocals of faith—that see the despair and the need of the hour, but also see, farther on, the patience of our God working out His plan in the world . . .

PETER MARSHALL

My prayer requests:	*God's answers:*

NEW YEAR'S EVE—OUR COVENANT GOD

December 31

God's Word to me: For this is My blood of the new covenant . . .
Matthew 26:28 (AMPLIFIED)
(Read also Exodus 24:6–8; Hebrews 8:7–13)

Prayer-meditation:

And now, beloved, let us bind ourselves with willing bonds to our Covenant God, and take the yoke of Christ upon us.

This taking of His yoke . . . means that we are heartily content that He appoint us our place and work, and that He alone be our reward.

Christ has many services to be done; some are easy, others are difficult: some bring honour, others bring reproach; some are suitable to our natural inclination and temporal interests, others are contrary to both. In some we may please Christ and please ourselves, in others we cannot please Christ except by denying ourselves. Yet the power to do all these things is assuredly given us in Christ, who strengtheneth us.

Therefore let us make the Covenant of God our own . . . and resolve in His strength never to go back . . .

And the Covenant which I have made on earth, let it be ratified in heaven.

JOHN WESLEY

My prayer requests: | *God's answers:*

DECEMBER SUMMARY

YEARLY SUMMARY

YEARLY SUMMARY

Alphabetical Index

Index of Scripture

407

Devotional Helps

A Diary of Private Prayer
By John Baillie
Oxford University Press,
Oxford

Adventures in Prayer
By Catherine Marshall
Hodder and Stoughton,
London

My Utmost for His Highest
By Oswald Chambers
Marshall, Morgan & Scott,
London

Streams in the Desert
By Mrs. Charles E. Cowman
Marshall, Morgan & Scott,
London

The Helper
By Catherine Marshall
Hodder and Stoughton,
London

*The Practice of the Presence
of God*
By Brother Lawrence
Hodder and Stoughton,
London

The Prayers of Peter Marshall
By Catherine Marshall
Fontana, London

The Screwtape Letters
By C. S. Lewis
Fontana, London

Your God Is Too Small
By J. B. Phillips
Epworth Press, London

THE HELPER

Catherine Marshall

The Helper, or Comforter, is the name Jesus used for the Holy Spirit when He began preparing His disciples for His death and resurrection. Catherine Marshall first discovered the Helper from a sickbed. Curious about the archaic term, Holy Ghost, she spent a summer searching the Bible for some explanation of that third member of the Trinity that no one really seemed to understand. She discovered that the Helper is a very real and potent entity – one that can affect our lives directly: "I discovered that the coming of the Holy Spirit to us and living within us is a gift, the best gift the Father can give us."

Here she shares the many experiences and discoveries she has made throughout her life about The Helper, offering a collection of 40 *helps* to provide direction and nourishment for the uncertain of faith, as well as assurance and strength for those whose lives have already been touched by the Holy Spirit. Each help contains vividly-written teaching, Scriptural references and Catherine's own seeking prayer.

"Cannot fail to meet our need and point us to God . . . Christian truth and literary skill."   *Church Times*

"Excellent."   *Life of Faith*

"Very readable . . . its inspirational quality will encourage and enlighten."   *The Expository Times*

BEYOND HEALING

Jennifer Rees Larcombe

A woman in the prime of life is struck down by a serious illness: surely God will heal her. But what if he doesn't?

When Jennifer Rees Larcombe learned she had a rare viral disease that threatened her life, she was forced to rethink the issue of healing. Where do faith, sin and God's will come in and why, despite so much prayer, does she remain ill?

Jennifer's stumbling progress towards an understanding of God's plans for her is recorded with disarming honesty, and her courage and humour will be an inspiration to all those who struggle in the face of suffering.

"This book should help many who are discouraged to discover that their lives have value to God."
Christian Weekly Newspapers

"Few will read it without being challenged and inspired."
Floodtide

"Beautifully written, and often heart-rending, this story will enlarge the heart and vision of caring Christians."
Evangelism Today